13th International Workshop on Finite State Methods and Natural Language Processing (FSMNLP 2017)

Umea, Sweden
4 – 6 September 2017

Editor:

Frank Drewes

ISBN: 978-1-5108-4746-0

Proceedings of the
13th International Conference on
Finite-State Methods and Natural Language Processing

FSMNLP 2017
Umeå, Sweden

Edited by
Frank Drewes

Proceedings of the 13th International Conference on Finite State Methods and Natural Language Processing, pages i–vi,
Umeå, Sweden, 4–6 September 2017. © 2017 Association for Computational Linguistics
https://doi.org/10.18653/v1/W17-4000

Introduction

These are the proceedings of the *13th International Conference on Finite State Methods and Natural Language Processing* (FSMNLP 2013), which was held from September 4 to September 6, 2017 in Umeå, Sweden, co-located with the *13th International Workshop on Tree Adjoining Grammars and Related Formalisms* (TAG+13), in order to foster the scientific exchange between the two research communities.

The conference series FSMNLP is the premier forum of the ACL Special Interest Group on Finite-State Methods (SIGFSM). It serves researchers and practitioners working on natural language processing (NLP) applications or language resources, theoretical and implementational aspects, or their combinations, that make use of finite-state methods.

FSMNLP 2017 received 17 submissions, each of which was carefully reviewed by at least three experts in the field. On the basis of these reviews the progeram committee selected eleven papers to be accepted for presentation at the meeting. Unfortunately, one of these papers had to be withdrawn later for budgetary reasons, which left ten papers for presentation and inclusion in this volume.

In addition to the regular papers, two invited talks were presented and three tutorials given:

Invited talk 1 Gregory Kobele.
Higher Order Structures in Minimalist Derivations
Invited talk 2 Ann Copestake.
Dependency Semantics and Composition

Tutorial 1 Johanna Björklund.
Minimization Techniques for Automata and Gammars
Tutorial 2 Sylvain Pogodalla.
Abstract Categorial Grammars as a Model of the Syntax-Semantics Interface for TAG
Tutorial 3 Laura Kallmeyer and Rainer Osswald.
Syntax-Driven Semantic Frame Composition in Lexicalized Tree Adjoining Grammars

I would like to express my deepest gratitude to all authors for submitting their papers to FSMNLP 2017, to the members of the program committee for their excellent work in selecting the best papers, and to the members of the research group *Foundations of Language Processing* at Umeå University for their help with the local arrangements.

Frank Drewes
chair

Organization

Program Chair

Frank Drewes

Invited Speakers

Ann Copestake, University of Cambridge
Gregory Kobele, University of Chicago and University of Leipzig

Tutorial Speakers

Johanna Björklund, Umeå University
Laura Kallmeyer & Rainer Osswald, Heinrich-Heine-Universität Düsseldorf
Sylvain Pogodalla, INRIA Nancy

Program Committee

Matthieu Constant, Université de Lorraine
Frank Drewes, Umeå University (chair)
Tim Fernando, Trinity College Dublin
Thomas Hanneforth, University of Potsdam
Colin de La Higuera, Nantes University
Måns Hulden, University of Colorado Boulder
Laura Kallmeyer, Heinrich-Heine-Universität Düsseldorf
Kevin Knight, University of Southern California/ISI
András Kornai, Budapest Institute of Technology & Hungarian Academy of Sciences
Marco Kuhlmann, Linköping University
Andreas Maletti, University of Leipzig
Mark-Jan Nederhof, University of St Andrews
Jakub Piskorski, Polish Academy of Sciences
Laurette Pretorius, University of South Africa, Pretoria
Giorgio Satta, University of Padua
Tatjana Scheffler, University of Potsdam
Heiko Vogler, TU Dresden
Bruce Watson, Stellenbosch University
Anssi Yli-Jyrä, University of Helsinki
Menno van Zaanen, Tilburg University
Lynette van Zijl, Stellenbosch University

Local Arrangements and Support

Suna Bensch
Henrik Björklund
Johanna Björklund
Petter Ericson
Anna Jonsson
Michael Minock

Table of Contents

Failure Transducers and Applications in Knowledge-Based Text Processing
Stoyan Mihov and Klaus U. Schulz 1

Transliterated Mobile Keyboard Input via Weighted Finite-State Transducers
Lars Hellsten, Brian Roark, Prasoon Goyal, Cyril Allauzen, Françoise Beaufays, Tom Ouyang,
Michael Riley and David Rybach 10

Harmonic Serialism and Finite-State Optimality Theory
Yiding Hao 20

Bounded-Depth High-Coverage Search Space for Noncrossing Parses
Anssi Yli-Jyrä 30

Multi-tape Computing with Synchronous Relations
Christian Wurm and Simon Petitjean 41

Finite-State Morphological Analysis for Marathi
Vinit Ravishankar and Francis M. Tyers 50

Word Transduction for Addressing the OOV Problem in Machine Translation for Similar Resource-Scarce Languages
Shashikant Sharma and Anil Kumar Singh 56

A FST Description of Noun and Verb Morphology of Azarbaijani Turkish
Razieh Ehsani, Berke Özenç and Ercan Solak 64

Evaluation of Finite State Morphological Analyzers Based on Paradigm Extraction from Wiktionary
Ling Liu and Mans Hulden 69

Evaluating an Automata Approach to Query Containment
Michael Minock 75

Conference Program

Monday, September 4, 2017

8:30–9:00   *Registration and Opening*

9:00–10:30   *Minimization Techniques for Automata and Gammars*
Tutorial by Johanna Björklund

10:30–11:00   ***Coffee Break***

11:00–12:30   *Abstract Categorial Grammars as a Model of the Syntax-Semantics Interface for TAG*
Tutorial by Sylvain Pogodalla

12:30–13:30   ***Lunch Break***

13:30–15:00   *Syntax-Driven Semantic Frame Composition in Lexicalized Tree Adjoining Grammars*
Tutorial by Laura Kallmeyer and Rainer Osswald

15:00–15:30   ***Coffee Break***

15:30–16:00   *Failure Transducers and Applications in Knowledge-Based Text Processing*
Stoyan Mihov and Klaus U. Schulz

16:00–16:30   *Transliterated Mobile Keyboard Input via Weighted Finite-State Transducers*
Lars Hellsten, Brian Roark, Prasoon Goyal, Cyril Allauzen, Françoise Beaufays, Tom Ouyang, Michael Riley and David Rybach

Tuesday, September 5, 2017

9:00–10:00   *Higher Order Structures in Minimalist Derivations*
Invited talk by Gregory Kobele

10:00–10:30   ***Coffee Break***

10:30–11:00   *Harmonic Serialism and Finite-State Optimality Theory*
Yiding Hao

11:00–11:30   *Bounded-Depth High-Coverage Search Space for Noncrossing Parses*
Anssi Yli-Jyrä

11:30–12:00   *Multi-tape Computing with Synchronous Relations*
Christian Wurm and Simon Petitjean

12:00–13:00   ***Lunch Break***

Tuesday, September 5, 2017 (continued)

13:00–13:30   *Finite-State Morphological Analysis for Marathi*
Vinit Ravishankar and Francis M. Tyers

13:30–14:00   *Word Transduction for Addressing the OOV Problem in Machine Translation for Similar Resource-Scarce Languages*
Shashikant Sharma and Anil Kumar Singh

14:00–14:30   *A FST Description of Noun and Verb Morphology of Azarbaijani Turkish*
Razieh Ehsani, Berke Özenç and Ercan Solak

14:30–15:00   ***Coffee Break***

15:00–16:30   SIGFSM Business Meeting

Wednesday, September 6, 2017

9:00–10:00   *Dependency Semantics and Composition*
Invited talk by Ann Copestake

10:00–10:30   ***Coffee Break***

10:30–11:00   *Evaluation of Finite State Morphological Analyzers Based on Paradigm Extraction from Wiktionary*
Ling Liu and Mans Hulden

11:00–11:30   *Evaluating an Automata Approach to Query Containment*
Michael Minock

Closing and Lunch

Failure Transducers and Applications in Knowledge-Based Text Processing

Stoyan Mihov
Institute of Information and
Communication Technologies
Bulgarian Academy of Sciences
25A, Acad. G. Bonchev Str.,
Sofia 1113, Bulgaria
stoyan@lml.bas.bg

Klaus U. Schulz
Centrum für Informations- und
Sprachverarbeitung (CIS)
Ludwig-Maximilians-Universität München
Oettingenstr. 67,
80538 München, Germany
schulz@cis.uni-muenchen.de

Abstract

Finite-state devices encoding lexica and related knowledge bases often become very large. A well-known technique for reducing the size of finite-state automata is the use of failure transitions. Here we generalize the concept of failure transitions for finite-state automata to the case of subsequential transducers. Failure transitions in the new sense do not have input but may produce output. As an application field for failure transducers we consider text rewriting with large rewrite lexica under the leftmost-longest replacement strategy. It is shown that using failure transducers leads to a huge space reduction compared to the use of standard subsequential transducers. As a concrete example we show how all Wikipedia concepts in an input text can be linked in an online manner with the Wikipedia pages of the concepts using failure transducers.

1 Introduction

A wellknown technique for reducing the size of large finite-state automata is the use of failure transitions (Aho and Corasick, 1975; Mohri, 1995; Crochemore and Hancart, 1997; Kourie et al., 2012; Björklund et al., 2014). While automata help to find strings in text, more advanced text processing tasks are often based on knowledge bases that provide information on characteristic portions of input texts (endings, words, phrases, etc.). Using this information, given input texts are translated to a new output form. Examples for this form of "text rewriting" include various forms of tagging, stemming, and (linguistic, semantic,..) annotation (KESA, 2016).

There are a number of efficient techniques for representing a finite dictionary of string entries with their corresponding mappings as finite-state machines and transducers (Mihov and Maurel, 2001; Daciuk et al., 2010). These techniques can produce a very compact representation of the dictionary. But in order to perform *text rewriting* based on the dictionary one has to traverse the dictionary starting from each text position and in addition apply a conflict resolution strategy. Therefore the time complexity for text rewriting is given by the length of the text multiplied by the maximal length of a dictionary entry.

Deterministic finite-state transducers offer an elegant framework to solve such a text processing task in a more efficient way. In (Mihov and Schulz, 2007) we considered "rewriting dictionaries", i.e. collections of strings where for each entry a replacement value (another string) is specified. We showed how to translate a given rewriting dictionary into a subsequential finite-state transducer that may be used to replace all occurrences of dictionary entries in a text by the replacements with only one traversal of the text by the transducer. Using this solution, the time complexity for text rewriting is linear in the length of the text and does not depend on the dictionary. For resolving conflicts between overlapping entries the leftmost-largest rewriting strategy is used. However, when using large rewriting dictionaries the size of the resulting subsequential transducer can become very large. A similar technique is used by Schmitz in (Schmitz, 2011) for constructing subsequential transducers that represent part-of-speech rules.

In this paper we introduce f-transducers, a new kind of deterministic transducer with failure transitions. A failure transition in our sense does not consume input, but it is essential that it may produce output. We show how to translate a given rewriting dictionary into an f-transducer that has the same functionality as the subsequential finite-

Proceedings of the 13th International Conference on Finite State Methods and Natural Language Processing, pages 1–9,
Umeå, Sweden, 4–6 September 2017. © 2017 Association for Computational Linguistics
https://doi.org/10.18653/v1/W17-4001

state transducer obtained in (Mihov and Schulz, 2007). In this way, a huge space reduction is obtained for large rewriting dictionaries. Since transitions in transducers come with output, saving transitions has even a larger benefit than in the automaton case. As a concrete application we consider a rewriting dictionary with 8 million entries where each title of a page of the English Wikipedia obtains a link text with anchor on the corresponding page of the concept. The f-transducer obtained from the translation runs over a text and replaces every mentioning of a Wikipedia concept by a link to the Wikipedia page. In this way, texts can be linked to the Wikipedia in an online-manner.

We start with formal preliminaries in Section 2. In Section 3 we introduce failure transducers. Section 4 presents the construction of f-transducers for text rewriting. The algorithm and complexity analysis of our construction is given in Section 5. Section 6 describes the annotation of concept names with Wikipedia. We finish with a short conclusion in Section 7.

2   Formal Preliminaries

An *alphabet* is a finite set Σ of symbols. Words of length $n \geq 0$ over an alphabet Σ are introduced as usual and written $a_1 \ldots a_n$ ($a_i \in \Sigma$). The unique word of length 0 is written ε. As usual, Σ^* denotes the set of all words over Σ. The concatenation of two words $u, v \in \Sigma^*$ is written $u \cdot v$ or uv.

Definition 2.1 A *deterministic finite-state automaton* is a tuple

$$\mathcal{A} = \langle \Sigma, Q, i, F, \delta \rangle$$

where Σ is an alphabet, Q is a finite set of states, $i \in Q$ is the start state, $F \subseteq Q$ is the set of final states, and $\delta : Q \times \Sigma \to Q$ is a partial function called the transition function. Let $\mathcal{A} = \langle \Sigma, Q, i, F, \delta \rangle$ be a deterministic finite-state automaton. The *generalized transition function* is the partial function $\delta^* : Q \times \Sigma^* \to Q$ inductively defined as

- $\delta^*(q, \varepsilon) := q$ for all $q \in Q$,

- $\delta^*(q, w\sigma) := \delta(\delta^*(q, w), \sigma)$ for all $q \in Q$, $w \in \Sigma^*$, $\sigma \in \Sigma$ such that $\delta^*(q, w)$ and $\delta(\delta^*(q, w), \sigma)$ are defined.

The *language accepted by* $\mathcal{A}$ is $L(\mathcal{A}) := \{w \in \Sigma^* \mid \delta^*(i, w) \in F\}$.

Definition 2.2 A *failure automaton* or *f-automaton* is a tuple

$$\mathcal{F}\mathcal{A} = \langle \Sigma, Q, i, F, \delta, f \rangle$$

where $\langle \Sigma, Q, i, F, \delta, f \rangle$ is a deterministic finite-state automaton and $f : Q \to Q$ is a partial function called the *failure function*. Let $\mathcal{F}\mathcal{A} = \langle \Sigma, Q, q_0, F, \delta, f \rangle$ be an f-automaton. The *completed transition function* $\delta_f : Q \times \Sigma \to Q$ is the least (with respect to $\subseteq$) function $\delta' : Q \times \Sigma \to Q$ such that $\delta'(q, \sigma) :=$

$$\begin{cases} \delta(q, \sigma) & \text{if } \delta(q, \sigma) \text{ is defined,} \\ \delta'(f(q), \sigma) & \text{otherwise, if } f(q) \text{ is defined.} \end{cases}$$

Similarly as δ and f also δ_f is a partial function. The *generalized completed transition function* is the (partial) function $\delta_f^* : Q \times \Sigma^* \to Q$ inductively defined as

1. for all $q \in Q$: $\delta_f^*(q, \varepsilon) := q$,

2. for all $q \in Q$, $u \in \Sigma^*$ and $\sigma \in \Sigma$ such that $\delta_f^*(q, u)$ and $\delta_f(\delta_f^*(q, u), \sigma)$ are defined: $\delta_f^*(q, u\sigma) := \delta_f(\delta_f^*(q, u), \sigma)$.

The *language* of the f-automaton $\mathcal{F}\mathcal{A}$ is defined as

$$L(\mathcal{F}\mathcal{A}) = \{w \in \Sigma^* \mid \delta_f^*(q_0, w) \in F\}.$$

Definition 2.3 A *subsequential transducer* is a tuple $\mathcal{T} = \langle \Sigma, Q, q_0, F, \delta, \lambda, \Psi \rangle$ where $\langle \Sigma, Q, q_0, F, \delta \rangle$ is a deterministic finite-state automaton, $\lambda : Q \times \Sigma \to \Sigma^*$ is a partial function called the *transition output function* and $\Psi : F \to \Sigma^*$ is a total function called the *state output function*. The domains of δ and λ must coincide. The *generalized transition function* δ^* is defined as above. The *generalized output function* is the partial function $\lambda^* : Q \times \Sigma^* \to \Sigma^*$ defined as

- $\lambda^*(q, \varepsilon) := \varepsilon$ for all $q \in Q$,

- $\lambda^*(q, w\sigma) := \lambda^*(q, w) \cdot \lambda(\delta^*(q, w), \sigma)$ for all $q \in Q$, $w \in \Sigma^*$, $\sigma \in \Sigma$ such that $\delta^*(q, w)$ and $\delta(\delta^*(q, w), \sigma)$ are defined.

The sets $L_{inp}(\mathcal{T}) := \{w \in \Sigma^* \mid \delta^*(q_0, w) \in F\}$ and $L(\mathcal{T}) :=$

$$\{\langle w, \lambda^*(q_0, w) \cdot \Psi(\delta^*(q_0, w)) \rangle \mid \delta^*(q_0, w) \in F\}$$

are respectively called the *input language* and the *function represented by* $\mathcal{T}$.

The notion of paths in a finite-state device and the length of a path are introduced as usual.

Definition 2.4 A *position* of $t \in \Sigma^*$ is a pair $\langle u, v \rangle$ such that $t = uv$. An *infix occurrence* (of the infix v) in $t \in \Sigma^*$ is a triple $\langle u, v, w \rangle$ such that $t = uvw$. An infix occurrence $\langle u_1, v_1, w_1 \rangle$ of the text t *blocks* another infix occurrence $\langle u_2, v_2, w_2 \rangle$ of t if $|u_1| < |u_2| < |u_1 v_1|$. In this case we write $\langle u_1, v_1, w_1 \rangle <_{ov} \langle u_2, v_2, w_2 \rangle$ and say that the two infix occurrences *overlap*. A set A of infix occurrences of the text t is said to be *non-overlapping* if two distinct infix occurrences of A never overlap.

Definition 2.5 Let A, B be two sets of infix occurrences of the text t. We define $AFTER(A, B) :=$

$$\{\langle u, v, w \rangle \in A \mid \forall \langle u', v', w' \rangle \in B : |u'v'| \leq |u|\}$$

$LEFTMOST(A) :=$

$$\{\langle u, v, w \rangle \in A \mid \forall \langle u', v', w' \rangle \in A : |u| \leq |u'|\}$$

$LONGEST(A) :=$

$$\{\langle u, v, w \rangle \in A \quad \mid \quad \forall \langle u', v', w' \rangle \in A : \\ |u| \neq |u'| \vee |v'| \leq |v|\}$$

Definition 2.6 Let A be set of infix occurrences of the text t. The *subset of leftmost-longest infix occurrences of A* is the set $LML(A) := \bigcup_{i=0}^{\infty} \mathcal{V}_i$ where $\mathcal{V}_0 := \emptyset$ and $\mathcal{V}_{i+1} :=$

$$\mathcal{V}_i \cup LONGEST(LEFTMOST(AFTER(A, \mathcal{V}_i))).$$

3 Failure transducers

Failure transducers, or f-transducers, represent a kind of deterministic transducer with a failure transition function. When applying a failure transition during text traversal, an empty part of the input is consumed. However, a non-empty output string may be produced. We start with an illustrating example.

Example 3.1 Consider the transducer in the upper part of Figure 1. Similarly as State 1, State 2 has outgoing transitions for input letters a, b, and c. Corresponding transitions lead to the same state. After introducing a failure transition from 2 to 1 with output D we can eliminate the standard transitions departing from State 2. The new transducer with failure transitions is shown below. Note that both the number of transitions and the size of the output representation has been reduced.

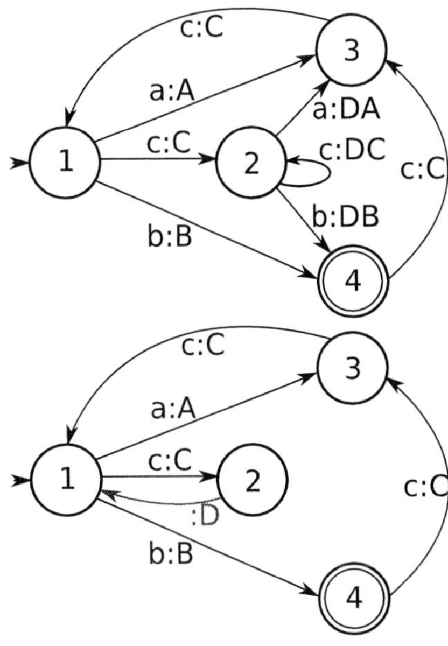

Figure 1: Illustration for Example 3.1: Compressing deterministic finite-state transducers using failure transitions.

When reading, say, symbol a in State 2, we follow the failure link to 1, producing output D. Then we use the a-transition from 1 to arrive at State 3. The total output is DA. The example might appear artificial since with other outputs we could not use the same technique. However, we shall see later that moving parts of the output to the failure transitions is often possible.

Transducers that are used for rewriting texts need to accept arbitrary strings. For this reason we do not introduce a special set of final states in our formalization of failure-transducers. As a matter of fact, generalizations are possible.

Definition 3.2 An *f-transducer* is a tuple

$$\mathcal{FT} = \langle \Sigma, Q, q_0, \delta, \lambda, \varphi, f \rangle$$

where Σ is a finite alphabet, Q is a set of states, $q_0 \in Q$ is the start state, $\delta : Q \times \Sigma \to Q$ is the deterministic transition function, $\lambda : Q \times \Sigma \to \Sigma^*$ is the transition output function, $\varphi : Q \to \Sigma^*$ is the *failure transition output function*, and $f : Q \to Q$ is the *failure transition function*. The following conditions must hold:

1. φ and f are partial functions such that $dom(\varphi) = dom(f)$.

2. the domains of δ and λ are identical, i.e., $dom(\delta) = dom(\lambda)$.

Definition 3.3 Let $\mathcal{FT} = \langle \Sigma, Q, q_0, \delta, \lambda, \varphi, f \rangle$ be an f-transducer. The *completed transition function* $\delta_f : Q \times \Sigma \to Q$ and the *generalized completed transition function* $\delta_f^* : Q \times \Sigma^* \to Q$ are defined as in Definition 2.2. The *completed transition output function* $\lambda_f : Q \times \Sigma \to \Sigma^*$ is defined as the least (with respect to $\sqsubseteq$) function $\lambda' : Q \times \Sigma \to \Sigma^*$ such that $\lambda'(q, \sigma) :=$

$$\begin{cases} \lambda(q, \sigma) & \text{if } \delta(q, \sigma) \text{ is defined,} \\ \varphi(q)\lambda'(f(q), \sigma) & \text{otherwise, if } f(q) \text{ is defined.} \end{cases}$$

The *generalized completed transition output function* $\lambda_f^* : Q \times \Sigma^* \to \Sigma^*$ is inductively defined as

1. For all $q \in Q$: $\lambda_f^*(q, \varepsilon) := \varepsilon$,

2. For all $q \in Q$, $u \in \Sigma^*$ and $\sigma \in \Sigma$:
$\lambda_f^*(q, u\sigma) := \lambda_f^*(q, u)\lambda_f(\delta_f^*(q, u), \sigma)$.

The *final state output function* $\Psi_f : Q \to \Sigma^*$ is defined as $\Psi_f(q) :=$

$$\begin{cases} \varepsilon & \text{if } f(q) \text{ is undefined,} \\ \varphi(q)\Psi_f(f(q)) & \text{otherwise.} \end{cases}$$

Let t be a text. The *output* of the f-transducer $\mathcal{FT}$ for input t is

$$O_{\mathcal{FT}}(t) := \lambda_f^*(q_0, t)\Psi_f(\delta_f^*(q_0, t)).$$

Informally, the way how an f-transducer processes a text t can be described as follows: starting from the start state and using the deterministic transition function δ we read the symbols of the text. The output at each transition is defined by the transition output function. When reaching a state p and a text symbol σ such that $\delta(p, \sigma)$ is not defined we apply a series of failure transitions until we arrive at a state p_n such that $\delta(p_n, \sigma) = p'$ is defined. The output produced on this intermediate walk has two parts. The first part is the concatenation of all failure transition outputs of the states $p, \ldots, p_n$ visited. The second part is given by the transition output of the final σ-transition. Finally, when arriving at state q at the end of the text, we apply a series of failure transitions, producing failure transition outputs, until we reach a state for which the failure function is not defined.

The following lemma shows that an f-transducer $\mathcal{FT}$ in a natural way defines a corresponding subsequential transducer with the same output function. The proof is a direct consequence of our definition of the output function $O_{\mathcal{FT}}$.

Lemma 3.4 Let $\mathcal{FT} = \langle \Sigma, Q, q_0, \delta, \lambda, \varphi, f \rangle$ be an f-transducer, let δ_f, λ_f, and Ψ_f as above. Then $\mathcal{T}_{\mathcal{FT}} := \langle \Sigma, Q, q_0, Q, \delta_f, \lambda_f, \Psi_f \rangle$ is a subsequential transducer and we have $O_{\mathcal{FT}} = O_{\mathcal{T}_{\mathcal{FT}}}$.

In what follows we consider failure transducers $\mathcal{FT}$ where each state q can be reached from the start state. The depth of a state $q \in Q$, denoted $d(q)$, is the minimal length of a path from start q_0 to q.

Definition 3.5 A *backwards f-transducer* is an f-transducer

$$\mathcal{FT} = \langle \Sigma, Q, q_0, \delta, \lambda, \varphi, f \rangle$$

such that for every $q \in Q$ we have $d(q) > d(f(q))$.

Proposition 3.6 *The time complexity (assuming a random access machine) for rewriting a word α of length n to a word β of length m by a backwards f-transducer is $O(n + m)$ and does not depend on the size of the transducer.*

The simple proof is omitted.

4 From rewrite dictionaries to f-transducers

As an application field for f-transducers we now look at text rewriting using dictionaries of a particular form.

Definition 4.1 (Mihov and Schulz, 2007) A *rewrite dictionary* is a pair $\mathcal{D} = (D, \Sigma)$ where Σ is an alphabet and D is a finite mapping of words over Σ. The mapping can be represented in the form

$$D = \{\alpha_i \mapsto \beta_i \mid 1 \leq i \leq k\}$$

such that $\alpha_i \neq \alpha_j$ for $i \neq j \in \{1, 2, \ldots, k\}$. Each string α_i is called an *entry* or an *original* of $\mathcal{D}$, and β_i is called the *replacement value* for α_i ($i = 1, \ldots, k$).

Definition 4.2 Let $t \in \Sigma^*$ be a text and $\mathcal{D} = (D, \Sigma)$ be a rewrite dictionary. A *rewrite occurrence* of $\mathcal{D}$ in t is an infix occurrence $\langle u, v, w \rangle_t$ such that $v \in dom(D)$. By $\mathcal{C}_t^{\mathcal{D}}$ we denote the set of all rewrite occurrences of D in the text t. The *global rewriting function associated with D* is the mapping $L(\mathcal{D}) : \Sigma^* \to \Sigma^*$ that given an input text t replaces each leftmost-longest infix occurrence of $\mathcal{C}_t^{\mathcal{D}}$ in t by the corresponding replacement value.

Example 4.3 (From (Mihov and Schulz, 2007)).
Let $\mathcal{D}$ denote the rewriting dictionary with alphabet $\Sigma := \{a, b, c, 1, 2, 3, 4, 5\}$ and mapping D of the form

$$
\begin{aligned}
(a &\mapsto 1) \\
(ab &\mapsto 2) \\
(abcc &\mapsto 3) \\
(babc &\mapsto 4) \\
(c &\mapsto 5)
\end{aligned}
$$

The leftmost-longest infix occurrences of $\mathcal{C}_t^{\mathcal{D}}$ in the text $t = abcbbbabccb$ are

$$
\begin{aligned}
&\langle \epsilon, ab, cbbbabccb \rangle \\
&\langle ab, c, bbbabccb \rangle \\
&\langle abcbb, babc, cb \rangle \\
&\langle abcbbbabc, c, b \rangle
\end{aligned}
$$

and $L(\mathcal{D})(t) = 25bb45b$.

We now describe a procedure for translating a rewrite lexicon $\mathcal{D}$ into a backwards f-transducer $\mathcal{FT}$ such that the global rewriting function $L(\mathcal{D})$ associated with $\mathcal{D}$ and $O_{\mathcal{FT}}$ are identical. The construction is a variant of the construction presented (Mihov and Schulz, 2007) for translating rewrite dictionaries into standard subsequential transducers. As in (Mihov and Schulz, 2007) we proceed in two steps.

Step 1. Given the rewrite lexicon $\mathcal{D}$, as in (Mihov and Schulz, 2007) we build a trie transducer $\mathcal{T}_D$ representing the domain of the lexicon mapping D. The final states of $\mathcal{T}_D$ correspond to the entries ("originals") of $\mathcal{D}$, and the failure transition output of each final state is defined as the image of the entry. The transition output for each transition is the empty string ε. The trie transducer thus represents the finite mapping D given by $\mathcal{D}$.

Step 2. The second step, where we build the failure transducer $\mathcal{FT}$ representing the global rewriting function for D, is based on a procedure where we visit the states of the trie transducer in a breadth-first manner, starting at the initial state q_0. We first complete the initial state q_0 adding loop transitions with any symbol $\sigma \in \Sigma$ such that there is no outgoing σ-transition from q_0 in the trie. The transition output for a loop transitions with symbol σ is σ. For all states q which are direct ancestors of q_0 i.e. such that $q = \delta(q_0, \sigma)$ we define $f(q) := q_0$ and $\varphi(q) := \sigma$ if q is not final. In case q is final the function $\varphi(q)$ is already defined.

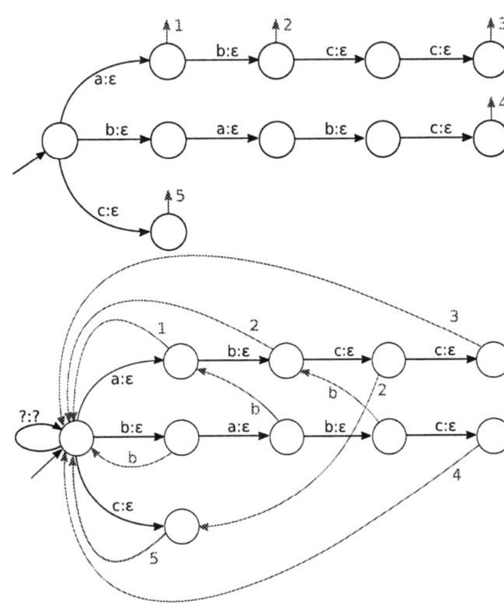

Figure 2: Trie-transducer (Step 1) and f-transducer (Step 2) obtained for the rewrite lexicon from Example 4.4.

Assume now that for the state $q \neq q_0$ we have already defined $f(q) = p'_q$ and $\varphi(q) = \gamma'_q$. Let $q' = \delta(q, \sigma)$ be an ancestor of q in the trie.

Case a. If q' is a final state of the trie transducer - i.e., if the failure transition output $\varphi(q')$ for q is already defined - we just define $f(q') := q_0$.

Case b. In the other case we define $f(q') := \delta_f(p'_q, \sigma)$ and $\varphi(q') := \gamma'_q \cdot \lambda_f(p'_q, \sigma)$.
The definition of δ_f shows that we find state $f(q')$ by starting from $f(q) = p'_q$ and applying failure transitions until we arrive at a state p_n such that $\delta(p_n, \sigma) = f(q')$ is defined.

Example 4.4 As an illustration for the translation of rewrite lexica into f-transducer we use the rewite lexicon from Example 4.3. The resulting trie transducer (Step 1) and f-transducer (Step 2) are shown in Figure 2. When processing text $t = abcbbbabccb$ we first read prefix abc with no output. Then two failure transitions produce output 25 before we can read the next letter b from the start. After reading t we have produced output $25bb45$ and the current state is the b-successor of the start. We have to add the final state output for this state, which is given by the failure transition output b (cf. Def. 3.3). The total output is $25bb45b$ as in Example 4.3.

Remark 4.5 For the following correctness proof we sketch Step 2 of the parallel construction of a subsequential transducer $\mathcal{T}$ in (Mihov and Schulz, 2007). Recall that in this case for each state q and

5

each symbol $\sigma \in \Sigma$ such that q does not have a σ transition in the transducer trie $\mathcal{T}_D$ a new σ-transition with suitable output needs to be added. For q_0 the procedure is as above (as for each state, also q_0 is made final). Consider a state $q_0 \neq q$ processed during Step 2. Let $plab(q) = a_1 \ldots a_r$ denote the label of the path π in the trie from q_0 to q. The *skip part of* $plab(q) = a_1 \ldots a_r$, denoted u_1, is:

1. a_1 if the state sequence π does not contain any final state of $\mathcal{T}_D$, and

2. $a_1 \cdots a_f$ ($f \leq r$) if this prefix of $plab(q)$ leads from q_0 to the last final state of π.

The *read part of* $plab(q)$ (denoted u_2) is the remaining part u_2 of $plab(q) = u_1 u_2$. Note that the read part is the empty word if q is a final state of $\mathcal{T}_D$ or if q is a direct successor of the start state q_0. The *failure state for* q is the state p' obtained when traversing the transducer $\mathcal{T}$ with the read part u_2, starting from q_0. The construction order guarantees that u_2 can be completely read in the preliminary version of the subsequential transducer $\mathcal{T}$ computed up to this point since the length of the read part u_2 is smaller than the length of $plab(q)$. The *output prefix for* q is the string γ' that represents the concatenation of (i) the output of the transducer $\mathcal{T}$ for the skip part u_1 (either a_1 or the substitute for the lexical entry $a_1 \cdots a_f$, cf. cases above) and (ii) the transition output of the transducer $\mathcal{T}$ for the read part u_2 when starting from q_0. With these notions, the processing of q can be described in the following way:

1. The state output for q is the concatenation of the output prefix γ' with the state output of the failure state p'.

2. If a new σ-transition from q is needed, the target state is the σ-successor of the failure state for q (it always exists since the failure state has smaller depth than q). The transition output for the new σ-transition from q is the concatenation of the output prefix γ' with the transition output of the transition with label σ from the failure state p'.

Correctness proof. Because of space limitations, an independent and fully selfcontained proof cannot be given here. However, using the correctness of the parallel construction in (Mihov

and Schulz, 2007) (shown in the paper) and Remark 4.5 we can prove correctness of the new construction. Let

$$\mathcal{FT} = \langle \Sigma, Q, q_0, \delta, \lambda, \varphi, f \rangle$$

denote the f-transducer obtained. Let

$$\mathcal{T} = \langle \Sigma, Q, q_0, Q, \delta_T, \lambda_T, \Psi_T \rangle$$

denote the subsequential transducer obtained from the construction described in (Mihov and Schulz, 2007). The following lemma captures some parallelisms between the two devices. We use the notation introduced in Definition 3.3.

Lemma 4.6 *1. For any state $q \neq q_0$ the state $f(q)$ is the failure state of q in the sense of Remark 4.5. We have $d(f(q)) < d(q)$.*

2. *For any state q and any letter σ we have $\delta_T(q, \sigma) = \delta_f(q, \sigma)$. Furthermore $d(\delta_T(q, \sigma)) \leq d(q) + 1$.*

3. *For any state $q \neq q_0$ the failure transition output $\varphi(q)$ is the output prefix $\gamma'(q)$ in the sense of Remark 4.5.*

4. *For any state q and any letter σ we have $\lambda_T(q, \sigma) = \lambda_F(q, \sigma)$.*

The proof for Lemma 4.6 is given in below. Looking at Part 3 of Lemma 4.6 it is simple to see that for each state q we have $\Psi_T(q) = \Psi_f(q)$. When we now compare the outputs produced for a text t by $\mathcal{T}$ and $\mathcal{FT}$ respectively we find, using Lemma 4.6, that

$$
\begin{aligned}
O_\mathcal{T}(t) &= \lambda_T^*(q_0, t) \cdot \Psi_T(\delta_T(q_0, t)) \\
&= \lambda_f^*(q_0, t) \cdot \Psi_f(\delta_f(q_0, t)) = O_{\mathcal{FT}}(t).
\end{aligned}
$$

In (Mihov and Schulz, 2007) it has been shown that $O_\mathcal{T}$ represents the global rewrite function $L(\mathcal{D})$ for the rewrite lexicon $\mathcal{D}$ under the leftmost largest strategy in the sense of Definition 4.2. Hence the same holds for $O_{\mathcal{FT}}$, which shows that the new construction is correct. $\square$

Proof of Lemma 4.6. Recall that for a state q, the length of the unique path from q_0 to q in the transducer trie is denoted $d(q)$. The proof is by induction on $d(q)$. If $d(q) = 0$ we have $q = q_0$. In this case, Claims 2 and 4 are obvious since we have $\delta_T(q_0, \sigma) = \delta_f(q_0, \sigma) =$

$$
\begin{cases}
\delta(q_0, \sigma) & \text{if } \delta(q_0, \sigma) \text{ is defined,} \\
q_0 & \text{otherwise.}
\end{cases}
$$

and $\lambda_T(q_0, \sigma) = \lambda_F(q_0, \sigma) =$

$$\begin{cases} \varepsilon & \text{if } \delta(q_0, \sigma) \text{ is defined,} \\ \sigma & \text{otherwise.} \end{cases}$$

There is nothing to show as to Claims 1 and 3.

For the induction step consider a successor state $q = \delta(q', \sigma')$. Let p' denote the failure state of q' in the sense of Remark 4.5. Let $p := \delta_T(p', \sigma')$. By induction hypothesis we have (i) $p' = f(q')$ and (ii) $\delta_T(p', \sigma') = \delta_f(p', \sigma')$. Furthermore $d(p') < d(q') < d(q)$ and $d(p) \leq d(p') + 1 < d(q)$.

We show Claim 1. If q is final, then $q_0 = f(q)$ is the failure state of q in the sense of Remark 4.5. In the other case the failure state of q in the sense of Remark 4.5 is $p = \delta_T(p', \sigma') = \delta_f(p', \sigma') = \delta_f(f(q'), \sigma') = f(q)$.

We show Claim 2. Let $\sigma \in \Sigma$. If $\delta(q, \sigma)$ is defined we have $\delta_T(q, \sigma) = \delta(q, \sigma) = \delta_f(q, \sigma)$. In the other case, first consider the case where q is final. Then q_0 is the failure state for q and $\delta_T(q, \sigma) = \delta_T(q_0, \sigma) = \delta_f(q_0, \sigma) = \delta_f(f(q), \sigma) = \delta_f(q, \sigma)$. By induction hypothesis $d(\delta_f(q_0, \sigma)) \leq 1$ and thus $d(\delta_T(q, \sigma)) \leq 1 < d(q) + 1$. If q is not final, then $p = \delta_T(p', \sigma')$ is the failure state for q. We have seen that $d(p) < d(q)$. By induction hypothesis $\delta_T(p, \sigma) = \delta_f(p, \sigma)$. Claim 1 shows that $p = f(q)$. Hence

$$\begin{aligned} \delta_T(q, \sigma) &= \delta_T(p, \sigma) = \delta_f(p, \sigma) \\ &= \delta_f(f(q), \sigma) = \delta_f(q, \sigma). \end{aligned}$$

We have $d(\delta_T(q, \sigma)) = d(\delta_T(p, \sigma)) \leq d(p) + 1 \leq d(q) + 1$.

We show Claim 3. If q is final, then $\gamma'(q) = \Psi_T(q) = \varphi(q)$ (note that $\Psi_T(q)$ is the state output for q in the transducer trie). In the other case, by induction hypothesis we have $\gamma'(q') = \varphi(q')$ and $\lambda_T(p', \sigma') = \lambda_F(p', \sigma')$. In this situation

$$\begin{aligned} \gamma'(q) &= \gamma'(q') \cdot \lambda_T(p', \sigma') = \varphi(q') \cdot \lambda_T(p', \sigma') \\ &= \varphi(q') \cdot \lambda_F(p', \sigma') = \varphi(q). \end{aligned}$$

We show Claim 4. Let $\sigma \in \Sigma$. If $\delta(q, \sigma)$ is defined we have $\lambda_T(q, \sigma) = \varepsilon = \lambda_F(q, \sigma)$. In the other case we have $\lambda_T(q, \sigma) = \gamma'(q) \cdot \lambda_T(p, \sigma)$ where $\gamma'(q)$ is the output prefix for q in the sense of Remark 4.5. Using Claim 3 and the induction hypothesis we see that

$$\begin{aligned} \lambda_T(q, \sigma) &= \varphi(q) \cdot \lambda_T(p, \sigma) \\ &= \varphi(q) \cdot \lambda_f(p, \sigma) = \lambda_f(q, \sigma). \square \end{aligned}$$

5 Implementation and complexity analysis

Algorithm 1 presents the pseudo-code of the construction. Clearly, the number of states of the f-transducer is bounded by $\|D_I\| + 1$ and the number of transitions is bounded by $2\|D_I\|$ and does not depend on the alphabet size, where $\|D_I\| = \sum_{\langle \alpha, \beta \rangle \in D} |\alpha|$. The complexity of the trie construction is $O(\|D\|)$, where $\|D\| = \sum_{\langle \alpha, \beta \rangle \in D} |\alpha| + |\beta|$. If each output string is represented in the standard way as a sequence of symbols, the space complexity of φ can get cubic in $\|D\|$. Using the technique for tree-based output string representation introduced in (Mihov and Schulz, 2007) the space complexity remains linear in $\|D\|$. In that case the space and time complexity of the proposed algorithm[1] is $O(\|D\|)$. In contrast, the space and time complexity of the construction presented in (Mihov and Schulz, 2007) is $O(\|D\| \cdot |\Sigma|)$ for an alphabet Σ. The complexity for rewriting a text t to t' is $O(|t| + |t'|)$.

6 Application for Online Hyperlinking Using Link Databases

Document repositories often come with a large number of internal or external links that lead from concepts (entities, references, etc.) mentioned in the text to other web pages. A well-known example is the Wikipedia[2]. On a Wikipedia page, all concepts of the text that are described in more detail in some other article of the Wikipedia are highlighted. When clicking at the concept the visitor is led to the relevant page of the Wikipedia, using an internal link (wikilink). In the same way, arbitrary texts can be linked with the Wikidedia.

To create a wikilink, concept names such as "United Kingdom" or "Kingdom University" mentioned in the text are replaced by anchor elements of the form

```
<a href="/wiki/United_Kingdom">
                United Kingdom</a>
<a href="/wiki/Kingdom_University">
                Kingdom University</a>
```

In order to automatize this form of hyperlinking, rewriting dictionaries may be used that list relevant concept names (e.g. "United Kingdom") together with the corresponding anchor elements

---

[1] Assuming that in the function `f-transducer` the loop transitions of q_0 in Lines 5-6 are not explicitly generated and the loops starting at Line 2 and Line 16 iterate only through existing transitions.

[2] http://en.wikipedia.org/wiki/Main_Page

Algorithm 1 Construction of an f-transducer for a given alphabet Σ and rewrite dictionary D.

```
Trie(Σ, D)                                    f-transducer(Σ, D)
@1   q₀ ← new_state()                         @1   ⟨Σ, Q, q₀, δ, λ, φ, f⟩ ← Trie(Σ, D)
@2   Q ← {q₀}                                 @2   for σ ∈ Σ do
@3   δ ← ∅                                     @3     q ← δ(q₀, σ)
@4   λ ← ∅                                     @4     if q = nil then
@5   φ ← ∅                                     @5       δ(q₀, σ) ← q₀
@6   for ⟨α, β⟩ ∈ D do                        @6       λ(q₀, σ) ← σ
@7     q ← q₀                                  @7     else
@8     for each symbol σ of α do              @8       if !φ(q) then
@9       p ← δ(q, σ)                           @9         push_queue(⟨q, q₀, φ(q)⟩)
@10      if p = nil then                       @10      else
@11        p ← new_state()                     @11        push_queue(⟨q, q₀, σ⟩)
@12        Q ← Q ∪ {p}                         @12   while not empty_queue() do
@13        δ(q, σ) ← p                          @13     ⟨q, p'_q, γ'_q⟩ ← pull_queue()
@14        λ(q, σ) ← ε                          @14     f(q) ← p'_q
@15      q ← p                                  @15     φ(q) ← γ'_q
@16    F ← F ∪ {q}                             @16     for σ ∈ Σ do
@17    φ(q) ← β                                 @17       q' ← δ(q, σ)
@18  return ⟨Σ, Q, q₀, δ, λ, φ, ∅⟩            @18       if q' ≠ nil then
                                               @19         if !φ(q') then
                                               @20           push_queue(⟨q', q₀, φ(q')⟩)
                                               @21         else
                                               @22           p'' ← p'_q
                                               @23           γ'' ← γ'_q
                                               @24           while δ(p'', σ) = nil do
                                               @25             γ'' ← concat(γ'', φ(p''))
                                               @26             p'' ← f(p'')
                                               @27           push_queue(⟨q', δ(p'', σ), concat(γ'', λ(p'', σ))⟩)
                                               @28   return ⟨Σ, Q, q₀, δ, λ, φ, f⟩
```

as a replacement. When processing a text with the rewriting dictionary, each occurrence of a concept name is replaced by the corresponding anchor element as a form of annotation. We note that the rewriting dictionaries used for automated hyperlinking are often extremely large.

Algorithm 1 has been applied for constructing a rewrite f-transducer for annotating texts with the anchor elements of practically all Wikipedia concept names in English[3]. The rewrite dictionary has $8,083,029$ entries and occupies 831 MB. The corresponding f-transducer was constructed by a not optimized implementation of Algorithm 1 using 64 bits for pointer, number and character representation. The resulting f-transducer has $69,037,940$ states and occupies 11.5 GB. On an Intel Xeon CPU at 2.40 GHz the construction time is 63 minutes. Using the constructed f-transducer, 100 MB of text are rewritten in approximately 19 seconds. This makes it possible to maintain huge knowledge bases in memory and rewrite texts in an on-line matter. In the same way, texts could be linked with any other collection of linked open data.

In order to compare the new construction with the construction presented in (Mihov and Schulz,

	time	size
subseq. transducer	283 s	1170 MB
f-transducer	12 s	79 MB

Table 1: Translation of a 5 MB rewrite dictionary into a text rewriting device. Construction times and sizes when using a subsequential transducer and an f-transducer.

2007) we used a 5 MB English correction dictionary with $220,231$ entries. All words in the correction dictionary are over the 26 lower case English letters. The rewrite f-transducer is constructed in 12 seconds and occupies 79 MB. The corresponding subsequential transducer is constructed in 283 seconds and occupies 1170 MB (cf. Table 1).

7 Conclusion

In this paper we introduced the concept of failure transducers. We presented in detail the construction of f-transducers for dictionary based text rewriting under the left-most-longest match strategy for conflict resolution. The advantage of the new construction compared to the method presented in (Mihov and Schulz, 2007) is space and construction time economy. The new construction

---

[3]There can be multiple concept names for one Wikipedia page.

avoids the increase in complexity which is caused by the enormous number of transitions needed for subsequential transducers when using rewrite dictionary over large alphabets. In our construction the number of ordinary transitions and the number of failure transitions of the f-transducer are bounded by the sum of the lengths of input words in the dictionary and do not depend on the alphabet size. This made it possible to construct an f-transducer for annotating all concept names of the English Wikipedia in a text in online manner on a personal computer. The same technique can be applied to similar forms of knowledge-based text rewriting. In this way, interesting items in input texts can be linked "on demand" in a user-driven online manner to distict targets such as lexica, authority pages, product catalogues and other resources.

References

Alfred Aho and Margaret Corasick. 1975. Efficient string matching: an aid to bibliographic search. *Communications of the ACM*, 18:333–340.

Henrik Björklund, Johanna Björklund, and Niklas Zechner. 2014. Compression of finite-state automata through failure transitions. *Theoretical Computer Science*, 557:87–100.

Maxime Crochemore and Christophe Hancart. 1997. Automata for matching patterns. In *Handbook of formal languages*, pages 399–462. Springer.

Jan Daciuk, Jakub Piskorski, and Strahil Ristov, 2010. *Scientific Applications of Language Methods*, chapter Natural Language Dictionaries Implemented as Finite Automata, pages 133–204. Imperial College Press.

KESA. 2016. Third international workshop on knowledge extraction and semantic annotation. In *Proceedings ALLDATA 2016 The Second International Conference on Big Data, Small Data, Linked Data and Open Data*, Lisbon, Portugal.

Derrick G. Kourie, Bruce W. Watson, Loek Cleophas, and Fritz Venter. 2012. Failure deterministic finite automata. In *Proceedings of Prague Stringology Conference*, pages 28–41.

Stoyan Mihov and Denis Maurel. 2001. Direct construction of minimal acyclic subsequential transducers. In *Proceedings of the Conference on Implementation and Application of Automata CIAA'2000*, number 2088 in LNCS, pages 217–229. Springer.

Stoyan Mihov and Klaus U. Schulz. 2007. Efficient dictionary-based text rewriting using subsequential transducers. *Natural Language Engineering*, 13(4):353–381, December.

Mehryar Mohri. 1995. Matching patterns of an automaton. In *Combinatorial Pattern Matching*, pages 286–297. Springer.

Sylvain Schmitz. 2011. A note on sequential rule-based pos tagging. In *Proceedings of the 9th International Workshop on Finite State Methods and Natural Language Processing*, FSMNLP '11, pages 83–87, Stroudsburg, PA, USA. Association for Computational Linguistics.

Transliterated Mobile Keyboard Input via Weighted Finite-State Transducers

Lars Hellsten[†], Brian Roark[†], Prasoon Goyal[*], Cyril Allauzen[†],
Françoise Beaufays[†], Tom Ouyang[†], Michael Riley[†] and David Rybach[†]

[†]Google, Inc.   [*]New York University

{lhellsten,roark,allauzen,fsb,ouyang,riley,rybach}@google.com
prasoongoyal13@gmail.com

Abstract

We present an extension to a mobile keyboard input decoder based on finite-state transducers that provides general transliteration support, and demonstrate its use for input of South Asian languages using a QWERTY keyboard. On-device keyboard decoders must operate under strict latency and memory constraints, and we present several transducer optimizations that allow for high accuracy decoding under such constraints. Our methods yield substantial accuracy improvements and latency reductions over an existing baseline transliteration keyboard approach. The resulting system was launched for 22 languages in Google Gboard in the first half of 2017.

1 Introduction

The usefulness of weighted finite-state transducers (WFSTs) has been well-documented for speech recognition decoding. Large component WFSTs representing a context-dependent phone sequence model (C), the pronunciation lexicon (L) and the language model (G) can be composed into a single large transducer ($C \circ L \circ G$, or CLG for short) mapping from context-dependent phone sequences on the input to word sequences on the output and optimized for efficient decoding (Mohri et al., 2002). In addition to forming the basis of numerous commercial and research speech recognition engines, this is the approach taken by the widely-used open-source toolkit Kaldi (Povey et al., 2011), which makes use of the OpenFst library (Allauzen et al., 2007) to represent and manipulate the WFSTs. Decoding via such an optimized graph permits the efficient combination of acoustic model scores of context-dependent phone sequences with the scores associated with larger (word n-gram) sequences contributed by the language model.

Speech is not the only uncertain input sequence modality requiring transcription to yield word strings – others include optical character recognition (OCR) and handwriting recognition. WFST-based methods have also recently been applied to soft keyboard decoding (Ouyang et al., 2017), where a sequence of taps or continuous gestures is decoded to the most likely word or word sequence. Unlike typing on a standard physical keyboard (such as a QWERTY keyboard on a laptop), ambiguity arises on a soft (on-screen) keyboard due to the relatively small size of the keyboard (e.g., on a smartphone) and the resulting imprecision of the tap or gesture. In such an approach, the same sort of off-line composition of weighted FSTs provides low latency decoding with a modest memory footprint, which is essential for on-device keyboard functionality. The FST-based decoder described in that paper was launched in the Google Gboard keyboard system in early 2017.

In this paper, we present methods for extending this finite-state decoding approach for mobile keyboard input to transliterated keyboards, where the keyboard representation differs from the output script. One very common scenario of this sort is the use of a standard QWERTY-style soft keyboard for entering text in a language with another writing system, typically because the Latin alphabet is simpler to represent on a compact soft keyboard. Systems for mapping from sequences of symbols in the target script to sequences of Latin symbols are known as *romanization*.

The most widely known romanization system is *Pinyin*, which is a fully conventionalized system for Chinese. For example, the word 水 (water) in Chinese is written as "shuǐ" in Pinyin. Romanization, however, is quite widely used around the world, with such writing systems as Arabic, Cyril-

Proceedings of the 13th International Conference on Finite State Methods and Natural Language Processing, pages 10–19,
Umeå, Sweden, 4–6 September 2017. © 2017 Association for Computational Linguistics
https://doi.org/10.18653/v1/W17-4002

Figure 1: Screen capture of a transliteration keyboard with a user's gesture trace for the target word.

lic, Greek and Thai. In many cases, unlike Chinese, there is no agreed upon standard romanization system, leading to an increase in ambiguity and noise when decoding to the target words in the native script. In this paper, we present a general transliteration approach applied to South Asian languages, transliterated from romanized input to a number of scripts, including Devanagari, Bengali and Perso-Arabic. Figure 1 shows a screenshot of a mobile transliteration keyboard for Hindi with the Devanagari script, showing the trace of the user's input gesture. While the user inputs romanized sequences, suggested word completions, as well as output strings, are in the target script.

In this context, we find that a WFST encoding of transliteration models allows for several optimizations that yield good accuracy under the strict resource and operating constraints of the on-device keyboard decoding. In what follows, we first provide background and preliminaries on Indic languages and their various scripts, as well as finite-state transducer terminology that will be used. We then describe our transliteration modeling approach and a number of WFST optimizations that we perform to achieve the accuracy, latency and memory usage operating points. Finally we present some experiments demonstrating the impact of the optimizations and comparing to an existing baseline. On Hindi and Tamil validation sets, we demonstrate strong word error rate and latency reductions versus an existing baseline. We conclude by presenting the various languages and associated scripts for which transliteration keyboards using this approach have so far been launched in Google Gboard, and by discussing future directions of this work.

2 Background and preliminaries

2.1 Indic scripts

While our approach is general enough to be broadly applicable to any transliteration pair, it is useful to have a running example, and since we later evaluate on South Asian languages, it makes sense to review Indic (or Brahmic) scripts here. We lack space to provide a full treatment of the scripts, but will provide details sufficient to understand our overall approach. We refer the interested reader to Sproat (2003) for further details.

Brahmic scripts are a class of writing systems that have descended from the Brahmi script and hence share certain characteristics. Well-known Brahmic scripts include Devanagari (the standard script for many languages, including Hindi and Sanskrit), Bengali, Gujarati and Tamil. Some South Asian languages have non-Brahmic native scripts, such as those that use the Perso-Arabic script (e.g., Urdu) and others that use modern scripts not descended from Brahmi (e.g., Ol Chicki for Santali). Still, Brahmic scripts are pervasive in South Asian languages, hence a key focus for keyboard entry in these languages.

While the Brahmic scripts can look very distinct, they have some central shared characteristics. The scripts are organized around what is termed an orthographic syllable (*akṣara*), which groups one or more consonants together with associated vowels. Each consonant has an inherent vowel, and other vowels – or different qualities of the vowels, such as nasalization, or also the absence of the inherent vowel – are indicated for that consonant via a mark or diacritic on the consonant. In most Brahmic scripts, vowels that are used independently of a consonant – e.g., word initially – have their own symbols. Finally, sequences of multiple consonants can be combined via ligatures.

For example, take the word "Sanskrit", written संस्कृत in Hindi. The initial syllable सं consists of the consonant स (s) which comes with its inherent vowel (sa), and an *anusvara* diacritic indicating that it is nasalized (san). This is followed by स्कृ (skr) which consists of four pieces combined into a single ligature: (1) a consonant स (s) with (2) a *virama* diacritic canceling its inherent vowel स्, followed by (3) another consonant क (k), which combines into the ligature स्क (sk)[1] plus (4) a vocalic 'r' diacritic, to yield the full glyph. Finally,

---

[1] Note the ligature omits the now-redundant *virama*.

11

the consonant त (t) completes the full word. Note that this word is encoded as a string of seven Unicode codepoints: स ं स ् क ृ त, and it is up to a rendering system to assemble these symbols into the appropriate two dimensional glyphs. See Sproat (2003) for more details.

2.2 Romanization and transliteration

Transliteration – converting from one writing system to another – is a widespread sequence-to-sequence mapping problem that arises in multiple contexts. For example, proper names must be represented in various writing systems, so transliterating names and places can be very important for translation or querying knowledge bases. While it is true that प्रणब मुखर्जी is the president of India and was born in पश्चिम बंगाल, it is more useful for those who do not read the Devanagari script to be presented with the information that Indian president Pranab Mukherjee was born in West Bengal. Hence, much work in transliteration is focused on translation and information retrieval (Knight and Graehl, 1998; Chen et al., 1998; Virga and Khudanpur, 2003; Haizhou et al., 2004; Gupta et al., 2014).

Knight and Graehl (1998) took pronunciation as a mediating variable in mapping between the two writing systems, and explicitly modeled grapheme-to-phoneme and cross-lingual pronunciation mapping in their model. For example, the probability of mapping to "Sanskrit" from संस्कृत would include probabilities for English pronunciation given the written form (e.g., S AE N S K R IH T), the Hindi pronunciation (S AH N S K R AX T) given the English pronunciation, and the Devanagari string given the Hindi pronunciation.

Haizhou et al. (2004) took a more direct modeling approach, simply modeling the observed mapping between one writing system representation and the other, with strong gains in accuracy. Under such an approach, transliteration is very similar to grapheme-to-phoneme recognition (g2p), where written representations of words (e.g., "sanskrit") are converted to pronunciations, represented by phone symbols ("S AE N S K R IH T" in the ARPAbet representation). This sort of pronunciation modeling is also a well-studied problem, being very important to both text-to-speech and speech-to-text, for deriving pronunciations of items that are out-of-vocabulary. A number of approaches have been used to model this conversion from one symbolic representation (letters) to another (phones) falling in rough monotonic alignment, including log linear models (Wu et al., 2014) and neural sequence models (Rao et al., 2015). Explicit finite-state methods such as Bisani and Ney (2008) and Novak et al. (2013; 2015) have been shown to be very competitive for g2p (Wu et al., 2014; Rao et al., 2015), and we adopt such methods here (see Section 3.1).

Romanization is the special case of mapping from other writing systems to the Latin script, often to permit easier keyboard input. As we can see from the Hindi example in the last section, the number of possible symbols in Brahmic scripts is large, due to the combinations of consonants and vowels via diacritics, and the multi-symbol ligatures. While keyboard layouts do exist for these scripts, transliteration from romanized input to the target Brahmic script is a common form of keyboard input, especially for mobile devices. As mentioned earlier, there are many romanization systems for these languages (in contrast to broadly conventionalized Pinyin systems), making this sort of transliteration keyboard challenging for Indic languages (Ahmed et al., 2011).

2.3 Weighted finite-state transducers

A weighted finite-state transducer $T = (\Sigma, \Delta, Q, I, F, E, \mathbb{K})$ consists of: input (Σ) and output (Δ) vocabularies; a finite set of states Q, of which (without loss of generality) one is the initial state I, and a subset of states $F \subseteq Q$ are final states; a weight semiring $\mathbb{K}$; and a set of transitions $(q, \sigma, \delta, w, q') \in E$, where $q, q' \in Q$ are, respectively, the source and destination states of the transition, $\sigma \in \Sigma$, $\delta \in \Delta$ and $w \in \mathbb{K}$. A weighted finite-state automaton is a special case where $\Sigma = \Delta$ and, for every transition $(q, \sigma, \delta, w, q') \in E$, $\sigma = \delta$. For the work in this paper, we make use of the OpenFst library (Allauzen et al., 2007) to encode and manipulate WFSTs, and, unless otherwise stated, use the tropical semiring for weights.

Encoding n-gram language models as WFSTs involves the use of failure-transitions (Allauzen et al., 2003) with a particular 'canonical' structure that corresponds to backoff smoothing. We use such an encoding for building word-based language models in the target language of the keyboard application, and also as an intermediate representation in the training of our transliteration transducer, as described in Section 3.1. For this language model training and encoding, we make use of the OpenGrm n-gram library (Roark et al., 2012), which provides counting, smoothing and pruning functions resulting in an OpenFst encoded model.

In speech recognition, a pronunciation lexicon, consisting of words found in the vocabulary of the n-gram model along with their pronunciations, can be compiled into a WFST with input vocabulary Σ of phones and output vocabulary Δ of words. When this lexicon L is composed with the n-gram model G, various optimizations can be carried out on the resulting transducer, to share structure and accrue costs as early as possible (Mohri et al., 2002). Similar optimizations are possible for keyboard models, where the input vocabulary Σ of the lexicon L is the letters that spell the words (see section 3.3).

2.4 WFST-based keyboard decoding

There are some differences between speech and keyboard decoding, which are presented in detail in Ouyang et al. (2017), and which we summarize here. The need for decoding arises in keyboard due to so-called 'fat finger' errors, where the actual point on the keyboard that was touched is not within the bounding box of the intended letter. The term for the sequence of letters corresponding to actual touch points is 'literal'. For example, on a mobile device, with a relatively small QWERTY keyboard, the literal string typed may be "sabsjriy" when the intended word was "sanskrit". In that example, three letters (b,j,y) adjacent to the intended letters (n,k,t) were touched. For possible intended keys, a spatial model provides likelihoods for touch points, via, for example, a Gaussian for each key centered at its central point, or perhaps a neural network learned from real touch data. As with speech, there is contextual dependency between adjacent keys, e.g., the distribution over touch points for a given key may depend on the previous key typed. The decoder takes as input a sequence of touch inputs on the device and combines the context dependent spatial model scores (analogous to the acoustic model in speech) with language model scores to determine the most likely intended word.

One key difference between speech and keyboard decoding is the privileged nature of the literal string in keyboard decoding. Free entry of text via a keyboard is by its nature an open-vocabulary interface, i.e., the user should be able to type whatever they want. The keyboard decoder must decide whether the most likely word according to its models is sufficiently more likely than the literal to warrant auto-correction. If the margin between the score of the best scoring candidate and the literal score falls below the margin required for correction, the literal is output, thus allowing for out-of-vocabulary (OOV) items to be typed.

In addition to touch typing, the WFST-based keyboard decoder also permits gesture input (Zhai and Kristensson, 2003), which involves tracing a path from the first letter of a word through all the letters to the final letter before lifting the finger. With gesture, there is no natural notion of literal string, since multiple words may have the same path, e.g., 'or' and 'our' on a QWERTY keyboard. As a result, OOV processing is restricted, much as with speech, and users must revert to touch typing to input OOVs. The same decoder, however, is used to combine scores from a gesture spatial model with the language model to find the most likely word string.

We train a weighted transducer to provide likely transliterations for unseen words and permit noncanonical transliterations for existing words, increasing uncertainty in the decoder. This is a particular challenge given the strict constraints that come with on-device keyboard modeling: latency can be no more than 20 msec, models must, in aggregate, be on the order of 10MB in size, and memory usage during decoding is strictly constrained.

3 Methods

3.1 Pair language models

Due to the latency and memory constraints of our keyboard application, we pursued methods that resulted in models that could be encoded in relatively compact WFSTs. As mentioned in section 2.2, explicit finite-state methods used for grapheme-to-phoneme conversion, such as Bisani and Ney (2008) and Novak et al. (2013; 2015) are very competitive. The starting point for all such methods is a simple per-symbol alignment of both the input string and the output string. Thus, for example, the word "phlegm" is pronounced F L EH M (again using the ARPAbet representation), and one natural alignment between the grapheme and phoneme sequences is: p:ϵ h:F l:L e:EH g:ϵ m:M

For transliteration, we can align a Devanagari

script Hindi word (संस्कृत) with its romanization (sanskrit or sanskrt), where we make use of the Unicode symbol sequence (सਂसਂकਂृत):

s:स a:ε n:ਂ s:स ε:ਂ k:क r:ਂ i:ε t:त

Note that symbols on either the input or the output may not directly correspond to a symbol on the other side (such as 'a', 'i' and ਂ in the above example), which we represent with an ϵ on the other side of the transduction. Given a lexicon of words and their pronunciations or transliterations (e.g., that 'sanskrit' is a romanization of संस्कृत), expectation maximization (EM) can be straightforwardly used to learn effective alignments of this sort.

Given an aligned sequence of input:output 'pair' symbols such as e:EH, we can build an n-gram model to produce joint probabilities over sequences of such pairs. We refer to these models as pair language models, though they are alternatively called joint multi-gram models (Bisani and Ney, 2008). By conditioning the probability of these input:output mappings on the prior context, the model appropriately conditions the probability of h:F on whether the previous mapping was p:ϵ. As stated above, results have shown these models yield very similar performance to more complex and compute-intensive modeling methods (Wu et al., 2014; Rao et al., 2015), and they can be directly encoded as WFSTs (Novak et al., 2013; Wu et al., 2014), making them excellent candidates for low-resource, low-latency keyboard decoder models.

One useful variant of these models are those that reduce or eliminate input and/or output ϵ symbols (insertions/deletions), by allowing the merger of multiple symbols on either the input or the output side. For example, for our pronunciation example above, we may derive an alignment ph:F instead of p:ϵ h:F, which can also be learned using EM (Novak et al., 2013; Novak et al., 2015). Given the structure of WFST-based language models (see section 2.3), which make use of ϵ-transitions to encode backoff, reducing the number of deletions and insertions is important when reducing epsilon cycles in the WFST.

3.2 Transliteration WFST optimization

Figure 2 shows a fragment of the bigram pair language model encoded as a WFST, with model weights not shown for clarity reasons. It is a bigram model, so the incoming arcs into any state are labeled with the same pair symbol, e.g., state 5

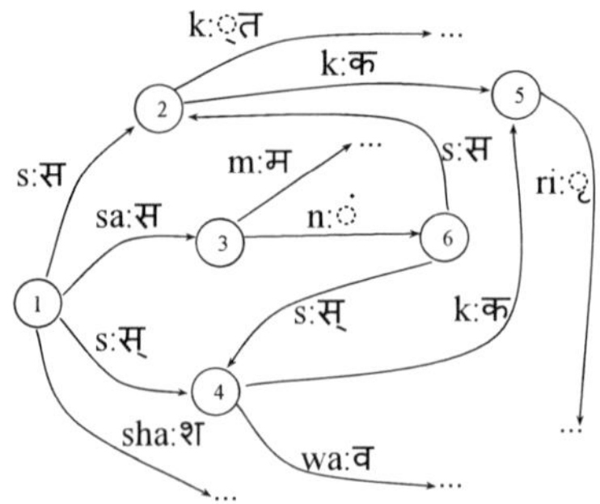

Figure 2: Fragment of the topology of a bigram pair language model, weights omitted for clarity.

has two incoming arcs, both labeled with k:क. The weights on each arc are the (typically negative log) probabilities of the pair symbols on the arcs given the state.

This WFST is an automaton over pair symbols, but we need a transducer mapping between Unicode codepoints on the input (QWERTY keyboard letters) and output (target script). If these were single symbol pairs, then converting to a transducer would be trivial: just change from a pair (encoded) symbol (k:क) to an input symbol (k) and an output symbol (क). However, as stated earlier, we merge symbols to reduce the number of insertions or deletions[2], as well as to increase the parameterization of the model, so the conversion to transducer is slightly more involved.

We illustrate our approach by considering the four arcs leaving state 1 in the pair language model automaton in Figure 2, all of which start with an 's' on the input side. Two arcs leaving state 1 have symbols consisting of multiple input Unicode symbols ('sa' and 'sha'); and one of the arcs leaving state 1 has a symbol consisting of multiple output Unicode symbols (स् which is two symbols स and ਂ). Figure 3 shows transducers that map these four pair symbols to their corresponding input and output strings. Figure 3a shows a transducer (call it I) with pair language model symbols (disambiguated with parentheses just for ease of visualization) on the output side and QWERTY key sequences on the input side. Figure 3b shows a transducer (call it O) with pair language model symbols on the input side and Devanagari Unicode symbols on the output side. For a pair language model P, we can derive our transliteration transducer T

---

[2]We also restrict the transducer to one insertion or deletion in a row, to avoid epsilon cycles.

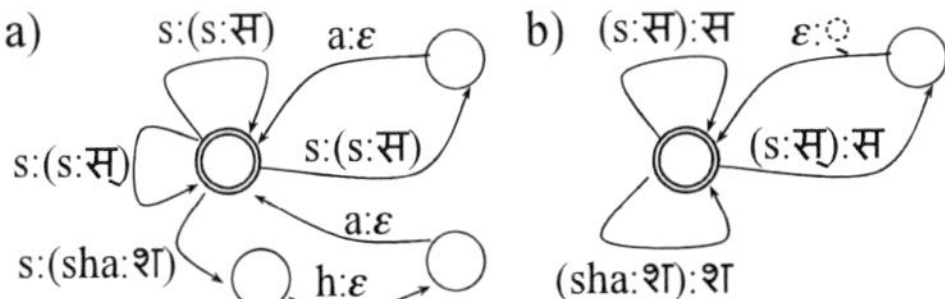

Figure 3: Fragments of transducers mapping a) from input Unicode symbols to symbols in the pair language model, and b) from symbols in the pair language model to output Unicode symbols. Parentheses in symbols are just to assist disambiguation in the figure.

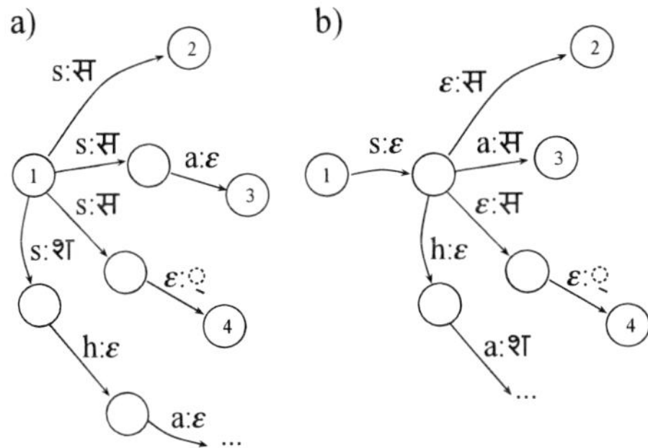

Figure 4: Illustration of conversion of pair language model to Unicode symbol transducer, showing state 1 of Figure 2: a) shows a direct conversion into single Unicode symbol transducer; b) shows a determinized structure which allows structure sharing and proper weight pushing. Numbered states are the same as in Figure 2 and unnumbered states are new.

by composing these together: $T = I \circ P \circ O$. The resulting transducer looks like the fragment shown in Figure 4a, where the original destination states from the pair language model in Figure 2 retain their numbers and new states are unnumbered. This is a simple conversion, with no structure sharing among arcs leaving the state, and the original model weights are accrued upon leaving state 1.

An alternate construction can be used, resulting in a transducer with structure like that shown in Figure 4b. This involves determinizing the input side of the transducer in Figure 3a mapping between input strings and pair language model symbols. As there are two paths with "s" on the input side (which is also a prefix of the other strings) this is not determinizable as is, much like pronunciation lexicons are not generally determinizable. We use a variant of the method presented in Mohri et al. (2002) to permit determinization in these cases. In their algorithm, they added an auxiliary phone symbol to the end of each pronunciation that indicated the word identity. In our case, as seen in Figure 5a, we create a transducer with each input symbol paired with ϵ, followed by an extra arc that

pairs an input ϵ with the full pair symbol. We then encode the transducer (treating the input:output as a a single symbol), determinize it, then decode it again to a transducer, resulting in the transducer in Figure 5b. We further reduce the size of this by combining sequential arcs labeled with $x{:}\epsilon$ and $\epsilon{:}y$ into a single arc $x{:}y$ in cases where the intermediate state has only one incoming and one outgoing arc. This results in the transducer in Figure 5c, which we can use in lieu of the transducer in Figure 3a to produce the final transducer, as illustrated in 4b.

While the structure sharing that results from this weighted determinization is important, its most important feature is the weight pushing that results. When building the encoded automaton in Figure 5a, we put the pair language model weight from the model on the first arc of each path, i.e., the arcs labeled S:ϵ in this example. When that automaton is determinized, the weights get pushed along the path, leaving only the minimum cost over all paths for which the transition is a prefix. This correct weight pushing of the transliteration cost yields major benefit during decoding.

One complication to keep in mind is that the transliteration cost provided by this model is based on a joint probability over input/output relations, not a conditional probability of the input given the output, which is what is needed (see Section 3.4).

3.3 L ∘ G optimization

In speech recognition, the $L \circ G$ transducer has phones on the input side and words on the output side. Unlike speech, however, in the current case the input symbols are individual Unicode symbols in the target script, the concatenation of which spells out the target word. Since the words can be inferred from the input symbols, we do not need to store the word labels explicitly; we project $L \circ G$ to its input labels (with an appropriate word boundary symbol to determine where such boundaries occur), and the decoder outputs concatenations of character label strings. Fig. 6 shows the structure of the optimized $L \circ G$ automaton.

The construction of $L \circ G$ is as follows. Starting with G, replace each non-backoff arc – i.e., arcs with word labels rather than ϵ – with a linear path corresponding to the word's symbols followed by the word end symbol (here </w>). Common prefixes of each such path leaving a state are merged to obtain a trie, backoff (ϵ) arcs are retained un-

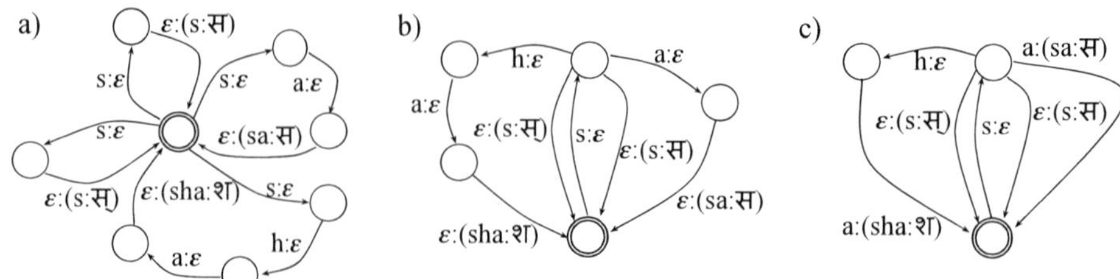

Figure 5: Fragments of transducers mapping from input Unicode symbols to symbols in the pair language model: a) with extra transition allowing for determinization; b) determinized on the encoded symbols; and c) combining sequential output and input ϵ transitions. Parentheses are just to assist disambiguation in the figure.

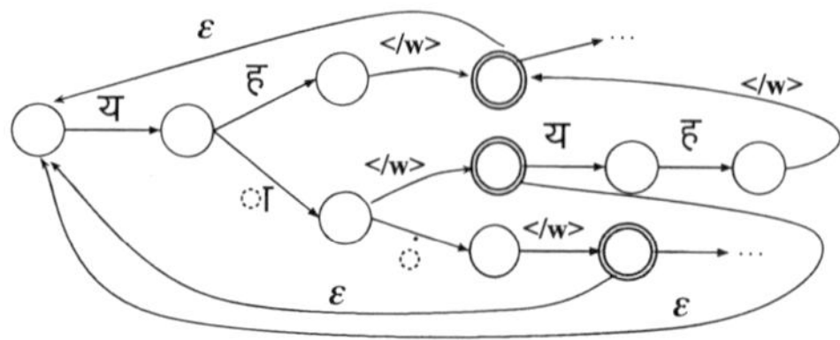

Figure 6: Illustration of the topology of $L \circ G$, for a fragment beginning at the unigram state containing the words या, यां, and यह, with the word end delimiter </w>. Weights are omitted.

changed, and weights are 8-bit quantized. Finally, the automaton is encoded using a variation of the LOUDS-based representation in Sorensen and Allauzen (2011). The topology of $L \circ G$ does not permit the use of the context trees from that representation. Instead, we store explicit 32-bit next state IDs for each backoff arc, indexed by rank in an indicator bit vector over states. We also store a bit vector indicating which states have a context transition arc, which must be an outgoing arc with the word end label. To find the destination state for these arcs, we recursively follow backoff arcs from the most recent word boundary state in the $L \circ G$ traversal until we're able to successfully find a context match.

Note that this structure is suboptimal in state/arc size, since common suffixes (tails) are not merged. But the topology allows for the LOUDS-based encoding which is more compact than a general compaction method could achieve on a more minimal but less regular topology.

3.4 Transliteration cost normalization

One key complication is the need for a conditional (not joint) transliteration model. The overall joint model of the words, transliterations, and touch points must be broken down into probabilities of: (1) the words (language model G); (2) the translit-

eration *given* the words; and (3) the touch points given the romanized symbols. Yet the transliteration model T is a joint model of aligned romanized and word strings. Thus each word requires an additional normalization factor.

We achieve this by dividing the probability of each w output by $L \circ G$ by the marginalization sum:

$$\mathcal{N}_w = \sum_{s,t \in T | \mathbf{concat}(t) = w} P_T(s, t)$$

where s and t are input and output sequences in the source and target scripts, respectively. Notice that in the log semiring, $\mathcal{N}_w$ is simply the weight of the shortest path in T that outputs an encoding of w. Thus, we project $T \circ L$ to output labels, determinize, invert weights, and compose the result with L to get a "conditional lexicon" L', such that $T \circ L' \circ G$ models the joint probability of a sequence of words and a corresponding transliteration.

We distribute this normalization factor via weighted determinization when building the trie leaving each language model state, as discussed in Section 3.3 and shown in Figure 6. Similar to the weight pushing that we get when determinizing the transliteration transducer, we put the negative normalization cost on the first arc of each path, then determinize, which distributes the weights correctly, and finally take the negative again to yield the correct normalization factor, which is now accrued incrementally at each character. Finally, to achieve full weight pushing in the $L \circ G$, we push the language model weights.

In addition to decoding sequences of taps and gestures, our keyboard application implements functionality that predicts the most likely completions and next word predictions (Ouyang et al., 2017). These require LM probabilities, which we can extract from $L \circ G$ by traversing arcs recursively until an arc with the word end symbol is encountered. However, note that the $L' \circ G$ FST described above has the transliteration normalization factor built into the cost. Thus we require a further modification to the next word prediction algorithm to remove the normalization factors: we store the normalization factors in a LOUDS trie (Delpratt et al., 2006) over the lexicon, and adjust the next word prediction costs correspondingly.

3.5 Decoder optimization

For conventional models, our keyboard decoder (Ouyang et al., 2017) uses on-the-fly composition of $(C \circ L)$ (statically composed) and G using look-ahead composition filters (Allauzen et al., 2009). Because of the ambiguity of transliteration, a statically composed $C \circ T \circ L$ is typically too large for a mobile application. For example, in a conventional Hindi model, $C \circ L$ contained fewer than 500k arcs, while incorporating T resulted in 35M arcs, requiring over 800 MB of storage. We addressed this by refactoring the composition so that a static $C \circ T$ is composed on-the-fly with a static $L \circ G$. With the optimizations discussed in previous sections, the former consists of approximately 100k arcs (1.7 MB), and the latter approximately 3M arcs (6.7 MB), which both fit within our constraints.

While the decoder graph optimizations achieve good model size characteristics, the overall number of states and arcs is much higher than in conventional models. If we use the same decoder meta-parameters as we do for a non-transliteration model, the decoder will search many more states, increasing latency and memory use. We employed the following optimizations, relative to non-transliterated models, to remain within our desired constraints:

Reduced beam width. The decoder prunes low-scoring hypotheses more aggressively.

Stricter error correction model. The decoder supports correction of insertion, substitution, and deletion errors (Ouyang et al., 2017). This model is assumed to be independent from the transliteration model, whereas in fact there is some overlap. For instance, doubling or interchanging vowels is one common source of transliteration ambiguity. We lowered probabilities in the edit model to help offset this.

Stricter spatial model. We used a slightly lower Gaussian variance in the tapping model, optimized for WER by sweeping over settings.

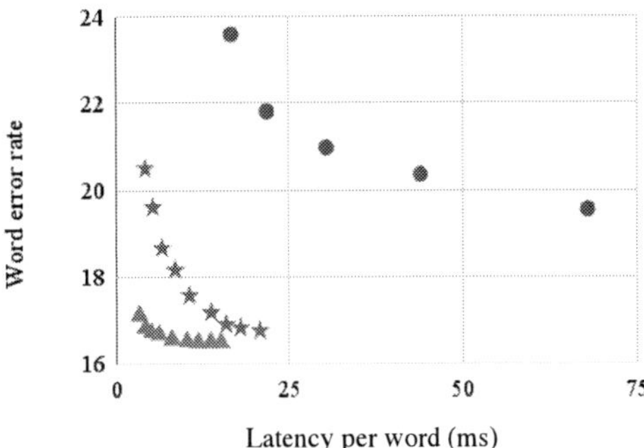

Figure 7: Sweep over beam sizes on Hindi dev set before and after transliteration transducer T weight pushing and $L \circ G$ weight pushing.

4 Experiments

4.1 Data

As is typical with non-transliterated systems, we use low order n-gram language models over a limited vocabulary. For the current study, vocabulary was 150k words and models were pruned trigrams with 750k n-grams.

Transliteration model training data consists of individual word transliterations for each native word in the vocabulary, collected from a small number (approximately 5) of speakers drawn from a larger overall pool of speakers. Each pair of (native word, transliteration) constituted one training instance used by the pair LM method described in Section 3.1. We ensured, using random sampling where necessary, that all words in the native vocabulary had the same number of training instances to avoid introducing bias.

Performance was evaluated on blind test datasets of tapped and gestured sentences in Hindi and Tamil (over 3000 words total for each input modality and language). In the data collection study, participants tapped and gestured sentences written in the native script on a smartphone QWERTY keyboard that produced no output, using their preferred transliteration. The prompts were sentences sampled from transcribed speech interactions. Participants were asked to type at a natural pace and not worry about fixing any mistakes, to collect natural errors and test the correction capability of the decoder and robustness of the transliteration modeling. We evaluate word error rate (WER), which is the number of errors divided by the number of reference words,

Language	$L \circ G$ size (MB)		
	standard	compact	LOUDS
Hindi	85.3	26.3	6.72
Tamil	126.5	37.1	9.80

Table 1: Size savings via LOUDS $L \circ G$ construction.

System	Hindi		Tamil	
	WER	LPC	WER	LPC
Baseline HMM system	19.5	3.0	26.2	2.1
WFST-based	16.4	0.5	22.6	0.2

Table 2: Word error rate (WER) and latency per character (LPC) results on blind test sets.

presented as a percentage.

The baseline system in our experiments comes from the Google Indic Keyboard, an existing product with between 50 and 100 million installations from the Google Play Store. It uses an HMM-based decoder, with a standard n-gram language model and a transliteration component consisting of conditional probability distributions $P(s \mid t)$ trained using the EM algorithm over a set of sub-word (primarily syllable) transliteration rules. The sub-word transliteration probabilities are assumed to be independent, in contrast to our approach. For this study, its language model and transliteration training data were identical to our system.

4.2 WFST optimizations

Table 1 presents the size in megabytes of the $L \circ G$ compiled in the standard way, with a general method of compression (compact), and with the specialized LOUDS format.

Figure 7 presents a sweep over beam search parameters on the Hindi dev set, for identical models compiled with and without weight pushing. As can be seen from that plot, with both transliteration transducer optimization (section 3.2) and $L \circ G$ optimization (section 3.3), very large latency reductions were achieved versus the unoptimized system, yielding the lowest word error rate along with the lowest latencies.[3] Due to these optimizations, low word error rates are achieved within the latency constraints imposed by the application.

4.3 Blind test evaluation

After setting meta-parameters on the development set for Hindi, we ran the decoder on blind test sets for both Hindi and Tamil. Table 2 presents a comparison between the WFST-based decoder and a baseline system.

5 Summary and future directions

We have presented a WFST-based approach to transliteration support in keyboards on mobile de-

Language	Script	Language	Script
Assamese	Bengali	Manipuri	Manipuri
Bengali	Bengali	Marathi	Marathi
Bodo	Bengali,	Nepali	Nepali
	Devanagari	Odia	Odia
Dogri	Devanagari,	Punjabi	Gurmukhi,
	Perso-Arabic		Perso-Arabic
Gujurati	Gujurati	Sanskrit	Devanagari
Hindi	Devanagari	Santali	Ol Chiki
Kannada	Kannada	Sindhi	Devanagari,
Kashmiri	Devanagari,		Perso-Arabic
	Perso-Arabic	Tamil	Tamil
Konkani	Devanagari	Telugu	Telugu
Maithili	Devanagari	Urdu	Perso-Arabic
Malayalam	Malayalam		

Table 3: Languages and scripts launched in GBoard using the methods presented in this paper.

vices, with specific results in South Asian languages. The presented WFST optimization methods yielded very large model size reductions, critical for on-device models. We also presented weight pushing approaches that yielded large speedups in decoding, with a commensurate reduction in active memory usage. The resulting system achieves large accuracy improvements in addition to strong latency reductions.

This approach has been used to build transliteration keyboard systems for the 22 languages shown in Table 3, some of which can be transliterated to different scripts. These keyboards were launched as part of Google Gboard in the first half of 2017. We continue to investigate new methods for training such models, including jointly training target script language models and transliteration models.

Acknowledgments

Thanks to Daan van Esch, Elnaz Sarbar and Cory Massaro for invaluable support with data curation; to Richard Sproat for useful guidance at the outset of this project and helpful perspectives throughout; and to Yuanbo Zhang for helping understand the Indic IME approach and facilitating direct comparisons of the approaches.

---

[3] Active memory usage is highly correlated with latency – being due to decoder search – hence we do not show that plot, though it shows a similar trend.

References

Umair Z Ahmed, Kalika Bali, Monojit Choudhury, and Sowmya VB. 2011. Challenges in designing input method editors for Indian languages: The role of word-origin and context. *Workshop on Advances in Text Input Methods (WTIM 2011)*, pages 1–9.

Cyril Allauzen, Mehryar Mohri, and Brian Roark. 2003. Generalized algorithms for constructing statistical language models. In *Proceedings of the 41st Annual Meeting on Association for Computational Linguistics*, pages 40–47.

Cyril Allauzen, Michael Riley, Johan Schalkwyk, Wojciech Skut, and Mehryar Mohri. 2007. OpenFst: A general and efficient weighted finite-state transducer library. In *Implementation and Application of Automata*, pages 11–23. Springer.

Cyril Allauzen, Michael Riley, and Johan Schalkwyk. 2009. A generalized composition algorithm for weighted finite-state transducers. In *Proceedings of Interspeech*, pages 1203–1206.

Maximilian Bisani and Hermann Ney. 2008. Joint-sequence models for grapheme-to-phoneme conversion. *Speech Communication*, 50(5):434–451.

Hsin-Hsi Chen, Sheng-Jie Hueng, Yung-Wei Ding, and Shih-Chung Tsai. 1998. Proper name translation in cross-language information retrieval. In *Proceedings of the 36th Annual Meeting of the Association for Computational Linguistics and 17th International Conference on Computational Linguistics-Volume 1*, pages 232–236. Association for Computational Linguistics.

O'Neil Delpratt, Naila Rahman, and Rajeev Raman. 2006. Engineering the louds succinct tree representation. In Carme Àlvarez and María Serna, editors, *Experimental Algorithms: 5th International Workshop, WEA 2006, Cala Galdana, Menorca, Spain, May 24-27, 2006. Proceedings*, pages 134–145. Springer Berlin Heidelberg, Berlin, Heidelberg.

Parth Gupta, Kalika Bali, Rafael E Banchs, Monojit Choudhury, and Paolo Rosso. 2014. Query expansion for mixed-script information retrieval. In *Proceedings of the 37th international ACM SIGIR conference on Research & development in information retrieval*, pages 677–686. ACM.

Li Haizhou, Zhang Min, and Su Jian. 2004. A joint source-channel model for machine transliteration. In *Proceedings of the 42nd Annual Meeting on association for Computational Linguistics*, page 159. Association for Computational Linguistics.

Kevin Knight and Jonathan Graehl. 1998. Machine transliteration. *Computational Linguistics*, 24(4):599–612.

Mehryar Mohri, Fernando Pereira, and Michael Riley. 2002. Weighted finite-state transducers in speech recognition. *Computer Speech & Language*, 16(1):69–88.

Josef R Novak, Nobuaki Minematu, and Keikichi Hirose. 2013. Failure transitions for joint n-gram models and g2p conversion. In *Proceedings of Interspeech*.

Josef Robert Novak, Nobuaki Minematsu, and Keikichi Hirose. 2015. Phonetisaurus: Exploring grapheme-to-phoneme conversion with joint n-gram models in the WFST framework. *Natural Language Engineering*, pages 1–32.

Tom Ouyang, David Rybach, Françoise Beaufays, and Michael Riley. 2017. Mobile keyboard input decoding with finite-state transducers. *arXiv preprint arXiv:1704.03987*.

Daniel Povey, Arnab Ghoshal, Gilles Boulianne, Lukas Burget, Ondrej Glembek, Nagendra Goel, Mirko Hannemann, Petr Motlicek, Yanmin Qian, Petr Schwarz, et al. 2011. The Kaldi speech recognition toolkit. In *IEEE workshop on automatic speech recognition and understanding (ASRU)*.

Kanishka Rao, Fuchun Peng, Haşim Sak, and Françoise Beaufays. 2015. Grapheme-to-phoneme conversion using long short-term memory recurrent neural networks. In *Proceedings of ICASSP*, pages 4225–4229.

Brian Roark, Richard Sproat, Cyril Allauzen, Michael Riley, Jeffrey Sorensen, and Terry Tai. 2012. The OpenGrm open-source finite-state grammar software libraries. In *Proceedings of the ACL 2012 System Demonstrations*, pages 61–66.

Jeffrey Sorensen and Cyril Allauzen. 2011. Unary data structures for language models. In *Proceedings of Interspeech*, pages 1425–1428.

Richard Sproat. 2003. A formal computational analysis of Indic scripts. In *International symposium on Indic scripts: past and future*, Tokyo.

Paola Virga and Sanjeev Khudanpur. 2003. Transliteration of proper names in cross-lingual information retrieval. In *Proceedings of the ACL 2003 workshop on Multilingual and mixed-language named entity recognition-Volume 15*, pages 57–64. Association for Computational Linguistics.

Ke Wu, Cyril Allauzen, Keith Hall, Michael Riley, and Brian Roark. 2014. Encoding linear models as weighted finite-state transducers. In *Proceedings of Interspeech*.

Shumin Zhai and Per-Ola Kristensson. 2003. Shorthand writing on stylus keyboard. In *Proceedings of the ACM SIGCHI conference on Human factors in computing systems*, pages 97–104.

Harmonic Serialism and Finite-State Optimality Theory

Yiding Hao
Department of Linguistics
Yale University
New Haven, CT, USA
`yiding.hao@yale.edu`

Abstract

This paper presents a new finite-state model of Optimality Theory (OT). In this model, two assumptions are imposed on the OT framework. Firstly, I adopt the Harmonic Serialism version of OT, in which output forms are derived from input forms via a series of incremental changes. Secondly, constraints are assumed to be *strictly local* in the sense that each markedness constraint specifies a set of banned sequences, each occurrence of which is penalized. I show that these two assumptions suffice to reduce the power of OT to rational relations.

1 Introduction

The seminal paper of Frank and Satta (1998) showed that grammars in the Optimality Theory (OT) framework can generate non-rational relations, but that a finite-state implementation is possible if each grammar specifies a bound on the number of violations that can be assigned by a constraint. Since then, various finite-state approximations of OT have been developed that achieve rationality by modifying the framework to reduce its computational power. Karttunen (1998), for example, implemented Frank and Satta's violation-bounded proposal by composing constraints using an operation called *lenient composition*. Improving upon this, Gerdemann and Van Noord (2000) and Gerdemann and Hulden (2012) developed a technique called *matching* that compares candidates based on the locations where violations are assigned. Eisner (2000) and Eisner (2002) propose a model called *directional OT* that prefers candidates whose violations are incurred as close as possible to the left or right boundary of the string. Finally, Riggle (2004) presents an algo-

rithm, called the *Optimality Transducer Construction Algorithm* (OTCA), that takes an OT grammar as input and produces a finite-state transducer that correctly computes the grammar if and only if the grammar defines a rational relation.

In this paper, I present a new formalization of OT that limits the generative capacity of OT in two ways. Firstly, I adopt the *Harmonic Serialism* (HS) version of OT. Whereas the standard version of OT simply maps each input to the candidate that best satisfies a sequence of constraints, HS produces outputs by effecting a series of incremental changes to the input. Secondly, I assume that all constraints are *strictly local*, in the sense that each constraint designates a set of marked sequences and assigns a violation for each occurrence of a marked sequence. I show that these two assumptions suffice to reduce the power of OT to rational relations.

The structure of this paper is as follows. In Section 2, I introduce technical definitions and terminology used in this paper. Section 3 motivates the use of strictly local constraints and HS as restrictions on OT. Section 4 presents a formalization of HS, and Section 5 presents a finite-state model of HS. Section 6 concludes.

2 Preliminaries

As usual, $\mathbb{Z}$ is the set of integers, and $\mathbb{N} \subseteq \mathbb{Z}$ is the set of non-negative integers. Unless otherwise specified, Σ denotes a finite alphabet, Σ^* denotes the set of all strings over Σ, and Σ^+ denotes the set of all nonempty strings over Σ. The special symbols $\rtimes$ and $\ltimes$ are assumed not to be elements of Σ. When used, these symbols represent the left and right boundaries of a string, respectively. The *length* of a string x is denoted $|x|$, and λ denotes the *empty string*, the string of length 0. Symbols from Σ are identified with strings of length 1, and

Proceedings of the 13th International Conference on Finite State Methods and Natural Language Processing, pages 20–29,
Umeå, Sweden, 4–6 September 2017. © 2017 Association for Computational Linguistics
https://doi.org/10.18653/v1/W17-4003

for any k, Σ^k denotes the set of strings of length k over Σ. For any strings $a, b \in \Sigma^*$, ab is the concatenation of a and b. If $A, B \subseteq \Sigma^*$, then $AB = \{ab | a \in A, b \in B\}$. If $a \in \Sigma^*$ and $B \subseteq \Sigma^*$, then $aB = \{a\}B$ and $Ba = B\{a\}$. A string a is a *substring* or a *subsequence* of b if one can write $b = lar$ for some $l, r \in \Sigma^*$.

For any sets A and B, $A \times B$ denotes the set $\{\langle a, b \rangle | a \in A, b \in B\}$. A *relation over A and B* is a subset $R \subseteq A \times B$. The *transitive closure* of a relation $R \subseteq A \times A$ is the smallest relation $\hat{R} \subseteq A \times A$ such that $R \subseteq \hat{R}$ and if $\langle x, y \rangle, \langle y, z \rangle \in \hat{R}$, then $\langle x, z \rangle \in \hat{R}$. For any relations R and S, the *composition* of R and S is the relation

$$R \circ S = \{\langle x, z \rangle | \exists y [\langle x, y \rangle \in S, \langle y, z \rangle \in R]\}.$$

A *finite-state transducer* is a 6-tuple $T = \langle Q, \Sigma, \Gamma, I, F, \delta \rangle$, where

- Q is a finite set of *states*;

- Σ is an alphabet called the *input alphabet*;

- Γ is an alphabet called the *output alphabet*;

- $I \subseteq Q$ is the set of *initial states*;

- $F \subseteq Q$ is the set of *final states*; and

- $\delta \subseteq Q \times (\Sigma \cup \{\lambda\}) \times (\Gamma \cup \{\lambda\}) \times Q$ is the *transition relation*.

The *extended transition relation* of T is the smallest set $\hat{\delta} \subseteq Q \times \Sigma^* \times \Gamma^* \times Q$ such that $\delta \subseteq \delta^*$; for every $q \in Q$, $\langle q, \lambda, \lambda, q \rangle \in \hat{\delta}$; and if $\langle q, x, y, r \rangle \in \hat{\delta}$ and $\langle r, a, b, s \rangle \in \delta$, then $\langle q, xa, yb, s \rangle \in \hat{\delta}$. The *behavior* of T is the relation $[T]$ such that $\langle x, y \rangle \in T$ if and only if for some $q \in I$ and $r \in F$, $\langle q, x, y, r \rangle \in \hat{\delta}$. A relation is *rational* if it is the behavior of a finite-state transducer.

A language L is k-*strictly local* if, for some set $S \subseteq (\Sigma \cup \{\rtimes, \ltimes\})^k$, $\rtimes L \ltimes$ is the set of strings such that every substring of length k is in S.

3 Restrictions on Constraints

Finite-state models of OT have typically achieved finite-stateness by imposing limitations on the power of constraints. The standard assumption, due to Ellison (1994), is that markedness constraints are finite-state mappings from strings to sequences of violation marks. The violation bound of Frank and Satta (1998) and Karttunen (1998) and the directional evaluation mechanism of Eisner (2000) and Eisner (2002) both refine the class

$aaabb$	DEP	ID	AGR	MAX
a. $aaabb$			*!	
b. $aaacbb$	*!			
c. $aaaaa$		*!		
☞ d. aaa				**
e. bb				***!

Figure 1: Tableau for a non-rational OT grammar

of possible constraints to a strict subclass of rational functions from Σ^* to $\mathbb{N}$.

In this paper, I propose to restrict constraints to a proper subclass of rational functions motivated by recent work on the *subregular hierarchy*. The subregular hierarchy consists of subclasses of regular languages and rational relations that characterize empirically attested patterns in phonology. Among these are the *strictly local* languages of McNaughton and Papert (1971), the *tier-based strictly local* languages of Heinz et al. (2011), and the *input strictly local* and *output strictly local* functions of Chandlee (2014). All four subclasses formalize the observation that markedness constraints in phonology generally designate a set of undesirable sequences as *marked*, and penalize strings that contain such sequences. Based on this intuition, I define a class of constraints called *strictly local constraints*.

Definition 1. A *strictly local constraint* is a function $c : \Sigma^* \to \mathbb{N}$ such that for some finite set $S_c \subseteq (\Sigma \cup \{\rtimes, \ltimes\})^*$, $c(x)$ is the number of unique decompositions $\rtimes x \ltimes = wyz$ such that $y \in S_c$. We say that c *bans* the sequence y if $y \in S_c$.

A strictly local constraint is a constraint of the form "assign one violation for every instance of s_1, s_2, ..., or s_n," where each s_i is a marked sequence. It can be easily shown that strictly local constraints are input strictly local functions from Σ^* to $\mathbb{N}$.

Unfortunately, strict locality of markedness constraints is not a sufficient condition for finite-stateness. Gerdemann and Hulden (2012) construct a non-finite-state OT grammar using only strictly local constraints as follows. The sole markedness constraint is AGR, which penalizes occurrences of the sequences ab and ba. AGR is outranked by the standard faithfulness constraints DEP and ID, which penalize insertion and substitution of symbols, respectively, while MAX, which penalizes deletion, ranks below all other constraints. This constraint ranking requires that

$aaabb$	DEP	ID	AGR	MAX
☞ a. $aaabb$			*	
b. $aaacbb$	*!			
c. $aaaab$		*!	*	
d. $aaab$			*	*!
e. $aabb$			*	*!

Figure 2: HS version of Figure 1

ab and ba sequences be destroyed by deleting seg-
ments. In order to remove all instances of ab or
ba, either all as must be deleted, or all bs must be
deleted. Between these two options, MAX favors
the one that involves less deletion. Thus, if the input has more as than bs, then the bs will be deleted;
otherwise, the as will be deleted. To illustrate, the
tableau in Figure 1 shows the derivation of the output aaa, obtained by deleting all bs from the input
$aaabb$.

Deleting the least frequent symbol from a string
is non-finite-state because such a mapping requires counting the number of occurrences of each
symbol. Since MAX adjudicates between the two
candidates obtained by deletion, MAX is responsible for counting in this example. While strict locality limits the power of markedness constraints,
this observation suggests that the power of faithfulness constraints should be limited as well. I
propose to do this using *Harmonic Serialism* (HS),
an alternate version of OT described in McCarthy
(2000). In HS, GEN only produces candidates that
differ from the input by one symbol. The winner
chosen by EVAL is fed back into the grammar until
a faithful mapping is obtained. To show how HS
can restrict the power of MAX, Figure 2 shows an
HS version of the tableau in Figure 1. Due to the
restricted power of GEN, only one deletion can be
performed at a time. The ab sequence in the input
$aaabb$ cannot be destroyed by deleting only one
symbol, so MAX simply chooses the faithful candidate. Since a faithful mapping is obtained, this
candidate is not fed back into the grammar.

4 Formalization of Harmonic Serialism

Having motivated the use of HS and strictly local
constraints, I now present a formal model of HS.

An HS grammar, like a standard OT grammar,
computes a relation $R \subseteq \Sigma^* \times \Sigma^*$ via the three
components GEN, CON, and EVAL. At the beginning of the computation, the grammar takes a
string x as input. GEN reads this input and returns

a set of *candidates*. CON assigns to each candidate a vector of natural numbers known as *violations*. Finally, EVAL, based on a linear ordering of
$\mathbb{N} \times \mathbb{N} \times \cdots \times \mathbb{N}$, reads the set of candidates and
their violations and returns the candidate y with
the optimal violation vector. If $y = x$, then y is
the output of the grammar. Otherwise, a recursive
call to the grammar is made with y as the input,
and the output from this call is the output of the
grammar.

As discussed in the previous section, HS differs
from standard OT in two ways. Firstly, recursive
calls to the grammar are not featured in standard
OT; instead, EVAL chooses the output in "one fell
swoop." Secondly, in HS, GEN is restricted so that
changes can only be made to the input "one at a
time," so that each call to the grammar produces an
optimal candidate that is only minimally different
from the input.

These ideas are formalized in the remainder of
this section. Let us begin with the notion of a
change. A single change to a string is defined as
insertion, substitution, or deletion of a single symbol in that string.

Definition 2. An *operation* is an ordered pair
$\langle x, y \rangle \in ((\Sigma \cup \{\lambda\}) \times (\Sigma \cup \{\lambda\})) \setminus \{\langle \lambda, \lambda \rangle\}$. An
operation $\langle x, y \rangle$ is an *insertion* if $x = \lambda$, a *deletion*
if $y = \lambda$, a *substitution* if $\lambda \neq x \neq y \neq \lambda$, and an
identity if $x = y$.

Definition 3. A pair $\langle a, b \rangle \in \Sigma^* \times \Sigma^*$ is an *application of operation* $\langle x, y \rangle$ if there exist $u, v \in \Sigma^*$
such that $a = uxv$ and $b = uyv$. An application
of an operation $\langle x, y \rangle$ is called a *change* when the
operation $\langle x, y \rangle$ is not specfied.

Strictly local constraints, defined in the previous section, formalize markedness constraints. To
treat faithfulness constraints, I adopt the standard
view that faithfulness constraints militate against
certain kinds of changes to the input. I will assume
that GEN is restricted so that on input a, GEN only
produces candidates b such that $\langle a, b \rangle$ is a change.
Since only one change can be made to a, faithfulness constraints can be seen as binary functions
that penalize applications of banned operations.

Definition 4. A *faithfulness constraint* is a function $f : \Sigma^* \times \Sigma^* \to \mathbb{N}$ such that for some set O_f of
operations not including identities, $f(a, b) = 1$ if
$\langle a, b \rangle$ is an application of some $\langle x, y \rangle \in O_f$, and
$f(a, b) = 0$ otherwise. If $\langle x, y \rangle \in O_f$, then we
say that f *bans* $\langle x, y \rangle$.

CON contains a set of constraints, which are assumed to be *ranked* with respect to one another. The ranking is represented here as a sequence of constraints.

Definition 5. For any strictly local constraint $c : \Sigma^* \to \mathbb{N}$, let c be extended to a function $c : \Sigma^* \times \Sigma^* \to \mathbb{N}$ defined by $c(x, y) = c(y)$. A *constraint ranking* is a sequence of functions $\langle c_1, c_2, \ldots, c_n \rangle$ where for each i, $c_i : \Sigma^* \times \Sigma^* \to \mathbb{N}$ is either a strictly local constraint or a faithfulness constraint. For any constraint ranking C, the number $k_C \geq 0$ is the length of the longest sequence banned by a strictly local constraint of C.

Among the candidates produced by GEN, EVAL chooses the one that violates the constraints the least. Given a constraint ranking $C = \langle c_1, c_2, \ldots, c_n \rangle$ and an input x, this is determined by considering for each candidate y the value $c_i(x, y)$. The winner chosen by EVAL is the one that minimizes this value for the most highly ranked constraints possible. To compare different candidates, I define here the notions of *cost*, *benefit*, and *harmonicity*.

Definition 6. The *cost* of a change $\langle x, y \rangle$ with respect to a constraint ranking $C = \langle c_1, c_2, \ldots, c_n \rangle$ is the vector

$$\mathfrak{c}_C(x, y) = \langle c_1(x, y), c_2(x, y), \ldots, c_n(x, y) \rangle.$$

The *benefit* of $\langle x, y \rangle$ is

$$\mathfrak{b}_C(x, y) = \mathfrak{c}_C(x, y) - \mathfrak{c}_C(x, x).$$

Definition 7. A vector $a = \langle a_1, a_2, \ldots, a_n \rangle \in \mathbb{Z}^n$ is *more harmonic* than a vector $b = \langle b_1, b_2, \ldots, b_n \rangle \in \mathbb{Z}^n$ if there exists j such that $a_j < b_j$ and for all $i < j$, $a_i = b_i$. We denote this by $a \succ_H b$. We write $a \succeq_H b$ if $a \succ_H b$ or $a = b$.

Putting these definitions together, an HS grammar is defined as a system, parameterized by a constraint ranking C, that takes a string as input and applies the change that results in the greatest benefit with respect to C. Recursion is performed until the most beneficial change is an identity.

Definition 8. An *HS grammar* is an ordered triple $\langle C, \mathcal{H}_C, \mathcal{H}_C^* \rangle$, where

- C is a constraint ranking;

- the relation $\mathcal{H}_C \subseteq \Sigma^* \times \Sigma^*$ is defined by $\langle u, v \rangle \in \mathcal{H}_C$ if and only if

$$\mathfrak{b}_C(u, v) = \max_y \mathfrak{b}_C(u, y),$$

  where max is taken with respect to $\succ_H$ over strings y such that $\langle u, y \rangle$ is a change; and

- letting $\hat{\mathcal{H}}_C$ be the transitive closure of $\mathcal{H}_C$, the relation $\mathcal{H}_C^*$ is defined by

$$\mathcal{H}_C^* = \{\langle x, y \rangle \in \hat{\mathcal{H}}_C \,|\, \langle y, y \rangle \in \mathcal{H}_C \}.$$

5 Finite-State Harmonic Serialism

The central result of this paper is that for any HS grammar $\langle C, \mathcal{H}_C, \mathcal{H}_C^* \rangle$, the relation $\mathcal{H}_C^*$ is rational. In section, I derive this result in two steps. Firstly, I construct a finite-state transducer whose behavior is $\mathcal{H}_C$. This shows that a single non-recursive call to a Harmonic Serialism grammar can be modelled as a rational relation. Secondly, I show that this transducer can be extended to a transducer whose behavior is $\mathcal{H}_C^*$.

5.1 $\mathcal{H}_C$ as a Rational Relation

This subsection describes a construction for a finite-state transducer that, for any constraint ranking C, computes $\mathcal{H}_C$. The construction relies on the property that the benefit of an application $\langle a, b \rangle$ of $\langle x, y \rangle$ can be computed using only information about a context of bounded size around the position of x in a and y in b. Since there are only finitely many such contexts, this locality property allows us to reduce the set of possible changes performed by $\mathcal{H}_C$ to a finite number of cases—one for each possible context. For each context, we can then construct a transducer that effects the most beneficial change for that context while ensuring that no context allowing for a more beneficial change is available. The union of all such transducers computes $\mathcal{H}_C$.

Let us now prove the locality property. To that end, I first introduce the definition of a context-sensitive rule, which captures the notion of an operation that only applies in a certain context.

Definition 9. A *rule* is an ordered quadruple $\langle x, y, c, d \rangle$, where $\langle x, y \rangle$ is an operation and $c, d \in (\Sigma \cup \{\rtimes, \ltimes\})^*$. We denote $\langle x, y, c, d \rangle$ by $x \to y \,/\, c\_d$.

Definition 10. An *application of a rule* $x \to y \,/\, c\_d$ is a pair $\langle a, b \rangle$ such for some $u, v \in (\Sigma \cup \{\rtimes, \ltimes\})^*$, $\rtimes a \ltimes = ucxdv$ and $\rtimes b \ltimes = ucydv$.

The locality property then states that every application of a rule with a sufficiently large context has the same benefit.

Proposition 11. *Let C be a constraint ranking, and suppose $\langle a_1, b_1 \rangle$ and $\langle a_2, b_2 \rangle$ are applications of a rule $x \to y \,/\, c\_d$. If $|c|, |d| \geq k_C - 1$, then $\mathfrak{b}_C(a_1, b_1) = \mathfrak{b}_C(a_2, b_2)$.*

Proof. Write $C = \langle c_1, c_2, \ldots, c_n \rangle$. We need to show that for each i,

$$c_i(a_1, b_1) - c_i(a_1, a_1) = c_i(a_2, b_2) - c_i(a_2, a_2).$$

Fix any $i \in \{1, 2, \ldots, n\}$. Note that $\langle a_1, b_1 \rangle$ and $\langle a_2, b_2 \rangle$ are applications of the same operation. Therefore, if c_i is a faithfulness constraint, then $c_i(a_1, b_1) = c_i(a_2, b_2)$. Since a faithfulness constraint cannot ban the application of an identity, $c_i(a_1, a_1) = c_i(b_2, b_2) = 0$. From this the equation above follows.

Now suppose c_i is a strictly local constraint. The equation above can then be rewritten as follows.

$$c_i(b_1) - c_i(a_1) = c_i(b_2) - c_i(a_2)$$

Let S_i be the set of sequences banned by c_i. For any string w, $c_i(w)$ is the number of occurrences of elements of S_i in w. Since b_1 and a_1, as well as b_2 and a_2, only differ by x and y, any occurrence of an element of S_i in b_1 but not a_1 or in b_2 but a_2 must contain the x that is replaced by y. Similarly, any occurrence of an element of S_i in a_1 but not b_1 or a_2 but not b_2 must contain the y that replaces x. Since $|c|, |d| \geq k_C - 1$ and $|s| \leq k_C$ for all $s \in S_i$, any occurrence of some $s \in S_i$ that includes either the x or the y must be a substring of cxd or cyd. Thus, we have

$$\begin{aligned} c_i(b_1) - c_i(a_1) &= c_i(cyd) - c_i(cxd) \\ &= c_i(b_2) - c_i(a_2), \end{aligned}$$

giving us the equation above. $\qquad\square$

Definition 12. Let C be a constraint ranking. The *benefit* of a rule $r = x \to y \, / \, c\_d$ with respect to a constraint ranking C, denoted $\mathfrak{b}_C(r)$, is defined by $\mathfrak{b}_C(r) = \mathfrak{b}_C(c'xd', c'yd')$, where c' and d' are c and d, respectively, with occurrences of $\rtimes$ and $\ltimes$ replaced by λ.

Using Proposition 11, we can now construct a transducer computing $\mathscr{H}_C$ by considering all possible rules $x \to y \, / \, c\_d$, where $|c| = |d| = k_C - 1$. For any input a, $\langle a, b \rangle \in \mathscr{H}_C$ if $\langle a, b \rangle$ is an application of the most beneficial rule that could be applied to a. Thus, for each rule r, we can construct a transducer that checks whether r is the most beneficial rule that is applicable to its input, and if so, apply r to its input. The following lemma gives us a way to check whether r is the most beneficial rule possible.

Lemma 13. *Let C be a constraint ranking, and suppose that $\langle a, b \rangle$ is an application of $r = x \to y \, / \, c\_d$, where $|c| = |d| = k_C - 1$. Suppose further that for all $y' \in \Sigma \cup \{\lambda\}$,*

$$\mathfrak{b}_C(x \to y' \, / \, c\_d) \preceq_H \mathfrak{b}_C(r).$$

Then, there is a set $F_r \subseteq (\Sigma \cup \{\rtimes, \ltimes\})^{2k_C - 1}$ such that $\langle a, b \rangle \in \mathscr{H}_C$ if and only if a does not contain any element of F_r as a substring.

Proof. Since $\langle a, b \rangle$ is an application of r, the length of a must be at least $|cxd| = 2k_C - 1$. Thus, for any $b' \in \Sigma^*$, $\langle a, b' \rangle \in \mathscr{H}_C$ only if $\langle a, b' \rangle$ is an application of a rule $r' = x' \to y' \, / \, c'\_d'$ with $|c'| = |d'| = k_C - 1$.

Such a rule r' is applicable to a if and only if a contains the substring $c'x'd'$. Thus, let us define F_r by

$$\begin{aligned} F_r = \{c'x'd' \,|\, &\mathfrak{b}_C(r') \succ_H \mathfrak{b}_C(r), \\ &|c'| = |d'| = k_C - 1\}. \end{aligned}$$

By hypothesis, $cxd \notin F_r$, so a rule more beneficial than r can be applied to a if and only if a contains a substring from F_r. But $\langle a, b \rangle \in \mathscr{H}_C$ if and only if no rule more beneficial than r can be applied to a, hence the lemma. $\qquad\square$

To use Lemma 13, we only consider rules $r = x \to y \, / \, c\_d$ such that no y' satisfies

$$\mathfrak{b}_C(x \to y' \, / \, c\_d) \succ_H \mathfrak{b}_C(r).$$

To check whether a rule r is the most benefical rule applicable to a string a, we simply construct the set F_r and check that a does not contain any element of F_r as a substring.

We are now ready to present the construction of a finite-state transducer for $\mathscr{H}_C$.

Theorem 14. *Let $C = \langle c_1, c_2, \ldots, c_n \rangle$ be a constraint ranking. Then, $\mathscr{H}_C$ is a rational relation.*

Proof. We need to construct a finite-state transducer T such that on input a, T outputs b if and only if $\langle a, b \rangle \in \mathscr{H}_C$. To do this, we consider two possible cases: either $|a| < 2k_C - 1$, or $|a| \geq 2k_C - 1$. In the first case, $\langle a, b \rangle$ is generally not an application of a rule $x \to y \, / \, c\_d$ with $|c|, |d| \geq k_C - 1$, so Proposition 11 does not apply. Instead, we simply observe that the relation

$$\{\langle a, b \rangle \in \mathscr{H}_C \,||\, a| < 2_C - 1\}$$

is finite, so it is automatically rational. Let T_0 be a transducer whose behavior is this relation.

Now, let us assume that $|a| \geq 2k_C - 1$. Then, a is an application of a rule $x \rightarrow y \mathbin{/} c\_d$ with $|c| = |d| = k_C - 1$, so we can use the technique discussed in this subsection. To that end, let R be the set of all rules $r = x \rightarrow y \mathbin{/} c\_d$ such that

- $|c| = |d| = k_C - 1$;

- $\mathfrak{b}_C(r) \succ_H \langle 0, 0, \ldots, 0 \rangle$; and

- there is no $r' = x \rightarrow y' \mathbin{/} c\_d$ such that $\mathfrak{b}_C(r') \succ_H \mathfrak{b}_C(r)$.

R is precisely the set of all rules r with $|c| = |d| = k_C - 1$, other than the identity, such that some application of r is in $\mathcal{H}_C$. For each $r \in R$, let F_r be defined as in Lemma 13.

For each rule $r = x \rightarrow y \mathbin{/} c\_d \in R$, we need to construct a transducer T_r that applies r if it is the most beneficial rule applicable to its input. As discussed earlier, this amounts to checking that the input does not contain any element of F_r as a substring, and then applying the rule. Observe that the set of strings without substrings from F_r forms a $(2k_C - 1)$-strictly local language S_r, so to achieve this effect, we can simply take a transducer applying the rule and restricting its domain to S_r. Let us call this transducer I_r, whose behavior is defined below.

$$[I_r] = \{\langle ucxdv, ucydv \rangle \mid ucxdv \in S_r,$$
$$y \in \Sigma \cup \{\lambda\}\}$$

To construct T_r, we simply add the boundary symbols $\rtimes$ and $\ltimes$ to the input, apply I_r, and then remove the boundary symbols.

$$[T_r] = \{\langle \rtimes s \ltimes, s \rangle \mid s \in \Sigma^*\} \circ I_r$$
$$\circ \{\langle s, \rtimes s \ltimes \rangle \mid s \in \Sigma^*\}.$$

Finally, to construct a transducer T computing $\mathcal{H}_C$, we simply take the union of all the T_rs, along with T_0 and the identity relation on any string for which no rule in R is applicable.

$$[T] = \left(\bigcup_{r \in R} [T_r] \right) \cup [T_0] \cup \{\langle s, s \rangle \mid \forall r \in R[s \notin S_r]\}$$

It is clear that $[T] = \mathcal{H}_C$, so $\mathcal{H}_C$ is rational. $\qquad\square$

5.2 Transducing Recursion

Having shown that $\mathcal{H}_C$ is a rational relation for any constraint ranking C, it remains to show that $\mathcal{H}_C^*$ is rational as well. Recall that the behavior of $\mathcal{H}_C^*$ is to repeatedly apply $\mathcal{H}_C$ until a fixed point is reached. Since rational relations are closed under composition, the naïve approach to transducing $\mathcal{H}_C^*$ is to take the transducer T constructed in the previous subsection and compose it with itself multiple times. This approach is not correct, however, because there is no bound on the recursion depth of an HS grammar. A string can, in principle, contain arbitrarily many instances of a sequence banned by a strictly local constraint, and such a string could require a recursive call for each instance of a banned sequence.

To address the problem of unbounded recursion depth, I rely on techniques from *regular model checking*, a discipline that analyzes automated systems with infinitely many state configurations and attempts to find the set of states reachable from the initial states. Under a paradigm introduced by Jonsson and Nilsson (2000) and Bouajjani et al. (2000), the set of possible states of a system are represented as a regular language, and the possible transitions between states are modelled as a rational relation. Finding the set of reachable states amounts to finding the transitive closure of the transition relation, since the transitive closure is exactly the relation obtained by applying the transition relation to itself arbitrarily many times. Accordingly, much has been written in the model checking literature about how the transitive closure of rational relations might be computed. Surveys of these results can be found in Nilsson (2000), Abdulla et al. (2004), and Abdulla (2012).

Using these techniques, we can take the transducer T computing $\mathcal{H}_C$ and compute its transitive closure $\hat{T}$. The effect of $\hat{T}$ is to apply $\mathcal{H}_C$ to a string arbitrarily many times, so $\hat{T}$ is able to handle the problem of arbitrary recursion depth.

The intuition behind the technique for computing the transitive closure is as follows. Consider the transducer T shown at the top of Figure 3. This transducer reads strings over $\Sigma = \{a, b\}$ and changes the first b to an a. This is done by having T begin in state 0, and enter state 1 when a b is read. Now, let us consider how a transducer computing $[T] \circ [T]$, which changes the first two bs in the input to as, might be constructed. Recall that on an input x, the *run* of T on x is the sequence $q_0 q_1 \ldots q_n$ of states that T enters into during its computation. On input x, T produces an output y by changing the first b of x to an a. To compute $[T] \circ [T]$, we must then feed y back into T,

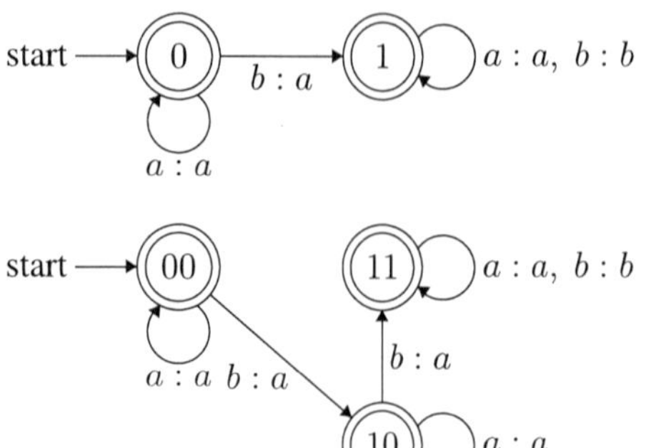

Figure 3: A transducer (top) and its composition with itself (bottom)

$$
\begin{array}{llllll}
x: & a & a & b & b & \ldots \\
\text{Run 1:} & 0 & 0 & 0 & 1 & 1 & \ldots \\
y: & a & a & a & b & \ldots \\
\text{Run 2:} & 0 & 0 & 0 & 0 & 1 & \ldots \\
z: & a & a & a & a & \ldots
\end{array}
$$

Figure 4: The runs of two applications of the transducer from the top of Figure 3

producing an output z. This produces another run $p_0 p_1 \ldots p_n$. The two runs are visualized in Figure 4, taking x to be a sample input beginning with $aabb$. A transducer T^2 computing $[T] \circ [T]$ can be constructed by stacking the two runs on top of one another. Each state of T^2 represents a *column* of the diagram in Figure 4—an ordered pair encoding the state of T during its first and its second iterations. Transitions can then be defined between the columns so as to match the behavior of T during its two passes. The resulting transducer T^2 is shown at the bottom of Figure 3. By inspection, it is clear that this transducer changes the first two bs of its input to as.

Let us now make these ideas explicit by defining the notion of a *column transducer*. This definition was introduced by Abdulla et al. (2002).

Definition 15. Let $T = \langle Q, \Sigma, \Sigma, \{q_0\}, F, \delta \rangle$ be a finite-state transducer such that $\langle x, y \rangle \in T$ implies $|x| = |y|$. The *column transducer for T* is the transducer $T^+ = \langle Q^+, \Sigma, \Sigma, q_0^+, F^+, \rho \rangle$, where $\langle q_1 q_2 \ldots q_m, a, b, r_1 r_2 \ldots r_m \rangle \in \rho$ if and only if there exist $a_0, a_1, \ldots, a_m$ such that $a = a_0$, $b = a_m$, and for each i, $\langle q_1, a_{i-1}, a_i, r_i \rangle \in \delta$.

Abdulla et al. (2002) show that for any transducer T computing a length-preserving relation, $[T^+]$ is indeed the transitive closure of $[T]$. How-

ever, this is not enough to show that the transitive closure of $[T]$ is rational. In the example of Figures 3 and 4, the transducer T^2 only computes two iterations of T, so the states of T^2 are columns of length 2. However, the column transducer T^+ has states of arbitrary length, so T^+ has infinitely many states, and is therefore not a finite-state transducer.

To remedy this, Abdulla et al. (2002), noting that different states often exhibit the same behavior, define an equivalence relation $\simeq$ on Q^+ in hopes that only finitely many columns in $Q^+/\simeq$ might be reachable.

Definition 16. Let $T = \langle Q, \Sigma, \Sigma, \{q_0\}, \{q_f\}, \delta \rangle$ be a finite-state transducer. A state $q \in Q$ is *left-copying* if $\langle q_0, x, y, q \rangle \in \hat{\delta}$ implies $x = y$. A state $q \in Q$ is *right-copying* if $\langle q, x, y, q_f \rangle \in \hat{\delta}$ implies $x = y$. A state is *non-copying* if it is neither left-copying nor right-copying.

Definition 17. Let $p, q \in Q^+$. We write $p \simeq q$ if there exist $m_1, m_2, \ldots, m_k, n_1, n_2, \ldots, n_k > 0$ and $q_1, q_2, \ldots, q_k \in Q$ such that

- $p = q_1^{m_1} q_2^{m_2} \ldots q_k^{m_k}$,

- $q = q_1^{n_1} q_2^{n_2} \ldots q_k^{n_k}$, and

- for each i, if q_i is non-copying, then $m_i = n_i = 1$.

Taking the quotient of Q^+ by $\simeq$ does not affect the behavior of T^+.

Theorem 18 (Abdulla et al. (2002)). *Define the quotient transducer of T by $T_\simeq = \langle Q^+/\simeq, \Sigma, \Sigma, [q_0^+]_\simeq, F^+/\simeq, \psi \rangle$, where*

$$
\psi = \{ \langle [p]_\simeq, a, b, [q]_\simeq \rangle \mid \langle p, a, b, q \rangle \in \rho \}.
$$

Then, $[T_\simeq] = [T^+]$ is the transitive closure of $[T]$.

This result shows that the transitive closure of $[T]$ is rational if only finitely many states in $Q^+/\simeq$ are reached. By inspecting Definition 17, we see that this is possible if each reachable column contains finitely many non-copying states, and if each column contains finitely many alternations between different copying states. Abdulla et al. (2003) introduce a technique known as *bi-determinization* for ensuring that the latter condition is always met, so the former condition is sufficient to ensure that the transitive closure of $[T]$ is rational.

We are now ready to use Theorem 18 to show that $\mathscr{H}_C^*$ is rational. To do so, we first need to modify the construction from Theorem 14 for the transducer T computing $\mathcal{H}_C$ so that $[T]$ is length-preserving. This can be done by padding strings with symbols that are treated like λs. Insertions are then performed by replacing these special symbols with symbols from Σ, while deletions are performed by replacing symbols from Σ with special symbols. This allows insertions and deletions to be simulated without changing the length of the input. Once T has been made to preserve length, we construct $T_\simeq$, and restrict its output to strings x such that $\langle x, y \rangle \in \mathcal{H}_C$ only if $x = y$.

Theorem 19. *Let C be a constraint ranking. Then, $\mathcal{H}_C^*$ is rational.*

Proof. Let $T = \langle Q, \Sigma, \Sigma, \{q_0\}, F, \delta \rangle$ be the finite-state transducer such that $[T] = \mathcal{H}_C$. We shall first show that the transitive closure of T is rational, and then use the transitive closure to construct a finite-state transducer whose behavior is $\mathcal{H}_C^*$.

Let $B = \{\texttt{i}, \texttt{d}\}$ be the special symbols used to pad strings so that $[T]$ can be made finite-state. Insertions are made by changing $\texttt{i}$s to other symbols, and deletions are made by changing symbols to $\texttt{d}$s. For any string $x = x_1 x_2 \ldots x_n$, define

$$\iota(x) = B^* x_1 B^* x_2 \ldots x_{n-1} B^* x_n B^*.$$

In other words, ι freely inserts special symbols to a string. Now, let us modify T by again considering the two cases where the length of T's input a is at most or greater than $2k_C - 1$. In the former case, for any $\langle a, b \rangle \in [T]$, write $a = uxv$ and $b = uyv$. We replace $\langle a, b \rangle$ with

- $\langle \iota(u)x\iota(v), \iota u \texttt{d} \iota v \rangle$ if $y = \lambda$,

- $\langle \iota(u)\texttt{i}\iota(v), \iota u y \iota v \rangle$ if $x = \lambda$, and

- $\langle \iota(u)x\texttt{i}\iota(v), \iota u \texttt{d} y \iota v \rangle$ if $x \neq \lambda$ and $y \neq \lambda$.

In the case where $|a| > 2k_C - 1$, let R be defined as in the proof of Theorem 14. Each rule $r = x \rightarrow y \,/\, c \_ d$ in R is replaced by

- $x \rightarrow \texttt{d} \,/\, \iota(c) \_ \iota(d)$ if $y = \lambda$,

- $\texttt{i} \rightarrow y \,/\, \iota(c) \_ \iota(d)$ if $x = \lambda$, and

- $x\texttt{i} \rightarrow \texttt{d}y \,/\, \iota(c) \_ \iota(d)$ if $x \neq \lambda$ and $y \neq \lambda$.

Let us call the set of these new rules R'.

In this modified version of T, the only modifications that could be made to the input are changing $\texttt{i}$s to alphabet symbols and changing alphabet symbols to $\texttt{d}$s. In particular, $\texttt{d}$s can never be

changed by T. Therefore, if T is applied to an input arbitrarily many times, for any i, the ith position only changes at most twice. This means that in the column transducer T^+, the column reached at the ith position can only contain at most two non-copying states, so in the quotient transducer $T_\simeq$, only finitely many states are reachable. Removing unreachable states makes $T_\simeq$ a finite-state transducer, so by Theorem 18, the transitive closure of $[T]$ is rational.

To complete the proof, let us use $T_\simeq$ to construct a finite-state transducer M for $\mathcal{H}_C^*$. Define the transducers E and D, which freely insert and remove padding symbols, respectively, as follows.

$$[E] = \{\langle x, y \rangle | x \in \Sigma^*, y \in \iota(x)\}$$
$$[D] = \{\langle x, y \rangle | y \in \Sigma^*, x \in \iota(y)\}$$

M must first insert padding symbols to its input, then apply $T_\simeq$, and then remove padding symbols. Afterwards, the range of these operations must be intersected with the set of strings such that the most beneficial change is the identity. Letting S_r be defined for each r as in Theorem 14, recall that this set of strings is precisely

$$S = \bigcup_{r \in R} S_r.$$

Since each S_r is regular, so is S. Therefore, we write

$$[M] = \{\langle x, y \rangle \in [D] \circ [T_\simeq] \circ [E] | y \in S\},$$

completing the construction. $\qquad\square$

6 Conclusion

In this paper, I have shown that the Harmonic Seralism version of Optimality Theory defines rational relations if markedness constraints are assumed to be strictly local. This was done by constructing a finite-state transducer relating each input with the winner chosen by EVAL after a single iteration of the grammar. This transducer was extended to a transducer that makes recursive calls to the grammar by relying on techniques from regular model checking for computing the transitive closure of rational relations satisfying certain conditions. The assumption that markedness constraints are strictly local allowed us to show that $\mathcal{H}_C$ is regular by partitioning the space of possible changes effected by the grammar into a finite number of cases. The limitation of GEN to "one change at a time" allowed us to construct the transitive closure of $\mathcal{H}_C$ in such a way that only finitely many states in the quotient transducer are reachable.

For computational phonology, this paper contributes a new finite-state model of OT that incorporates ideas from recent work on the subregular hierarchy and provides an example of how the property of locality could be exploited to restrict the power of OT to rational relations. The model presented here is also the first to achieve finite-stateness using restrictions on OT originating in the phonological literature: most markedness constraints proposed in OT analyses are indeed strictly local, and Harmonic Serialism was first introduced in the original manuscript of Prince and Smolensky (1993).

This paper also has implications for theoretical phonology. While Harmonic Serialism is generally known as a way to model phonological opacity, McCarthy (2000) mentions that in many cases, HS analyses are not distinguishable from standard OT analyses. On the other hand, the ability of HS grammars to make recursive calls is traditionally seen as a significant increase in the complexity of OT, so a standard OT analysis is usually preferable to a similar HS analysis. The proposal of this paper, however, provides evidence against that intuition: since standard OT with strictly local constraints is more powerful than rational relations, the finite-state model presented here shows that HS is weaker than standard OT in language-theoretic terms. Thus, this paper supports the viewpoint, originating from Moreton (1999)'s proof that the recursion of EVAL always converges to a fixed point, that HS is in fact *less* complex than standard OT. While the ability to feed the output of EVAL back into GEN seems to increase the power of OT, this increase in power is offset by the restriction of GEN to one operation at a time. The rationality of HS provides an interesting distinction between standard OT and HS, and presents motivation for further work on HS phonology.

To conclude, several issues should be addressed in future work on this topic. Firstly, the results presented in this paper are purely theoretical. An implementation of the two constructions described in Section 5 needs to be developed if the ideas from this paper are to be used in NLP applications. Secondly, while the class of strictly local constraints is motived in part by empirical studies regarding phonological patterns in natural language, many constraints found in OT fall outside of this class. Future work should determine the extent to which the power of constraints can be extended while still ensuring that HS grammars define rational relations. One possibility would be to extend strictly local constraints to a class of constraints corresponding to the tier-based strictly local languages. Finally, for the sake of formal completeness, many commitments were made in Section 4 in the development of the formal model of HS used in this paper. In particular, I have assumed that "one change at a time" means insertion, deletion, or substitution of a single symbol. I have also assumed that if a single iteration of EVAL chooses multiple winners, each of these winners is passed back to GEN independently. In reality, multiple proposals exist in the HS literature regarding the implementational details of the framework. By modifying the formalism of Section 4, further studies could investigate which of these details affect the generative power of HS, and which do not.

Acknowledgments

I would like to thank Ryan Bennett, Robert Frank, and the reviewers for their valuable feedback and discussion. Any remaining errors are my own.

References

Parosh Aziz Abdulla, Bengt Jonsson, Marcus Nilsson, and Julien d'Orso. 2002. Regular model checking made simple and effcient. In *International Conference on Concurrency Theory*, pages 116–131. Springer.

Parosh Aziz Abdulla, Bengt Jonsson, Marcus Nilsson, and Julien d'Orso. 2003. Algorithmic improvements in regular model checking. In *International Conference on Computer Aided Verification*, pages 236–248. Springer.

Parosh Aziz Abdulla, Bengt Jonsson, Marcus Nilsson, and Mayank Saksena. 2004. A survey of regular model checking. In *International Conference on Concurrency Theory*, pages 35–48. Springer.

Parosh Aziz Abdulla. 2012. Regular model checking. *International Journal on Software Tools for Technology Transfer (STTT)*, 14(2):109–118.

Ahmed Bouajjani, Bengt Jonsson, Marcus Nilsson, and Tayssir Touili. 2000. Regular model checking. In *CAV*, volume 1855, pages 403–418. Springer.

Jane Chandlee. 2014. *Strictly local phonological processes*. Ph.D. thesis, University of Delaware.

Jason Eisner. 2000. Directional constraint evaluation in optimality theory. *Proceedings of COLING*.

Jason Eisner. 2002. Comprehension and compilation in optimality theory. In *Proceedings of the 40th Annual Meeting on Association for Computational Linguistics*, pages 56–63. Association for Computational Linguistics.

T Mark Ellison. 1994. Phonological derivation in optimality theory. In *Proceedings of the 15th conference on Computational linguistics-Volume 2*, pages 1007–1013. Association for Computational Linguistics.

Robert Frank and Giorgio Satta. 1998. Optimality theory and the generative complexity of constraint violability. *Computational Linguistics*, 24(2):307–315.

Dale Gerdemann and Mans Hulden. 2012. Practical finite state optimality theory. In *FSMNLP*, pages 10–19.

Dale Gerdemann and Gertjan Van Noord. 2000. Approximation and exactness in finite state optimality theory. *arXiv preprint cs/0006038*.

Jeffrey Heinz, Chetan Rawal, and Herbert G Tanner. 2011. Tier-based strictly local constraints for phonology. In *Proceedings of the 49th Annual Meeting of the Association for Computational Linguistics: Human Language Technologies: short papers-Volume 2*, pages 58–64. Association for Computational Linguistics.

Bengt Jonsson and Marcus Nilsson. 2000. Transitive closures of regular relations for verifying infinite-state systems. In *TACAS*, volume 1785, pages 220–234. Springer.

Lauri Karttunen. 1998. The proper treatment of optimality in computational phonology: plenary talk. In *Proceedings of the International Workshop on Finite State Methods in Natural Language Processing*, pages 1–12. Association for Computational Linguistics.

John J McCarthy. 2000. Harmonic serialism and parallelism.

Robert McNaughton and Seymour A Papert. 1971. *Counter-Free Automata (MIT research monograph no. 65)*. The MIT Press.

Elliott Moreton. 1999. Non-computable functions in optimality theory.

Marcus Nilsson. 2000. *Regular model checking*. Ph.D. thesis, Uppsala universitet.

Alan Prince and Paul Smolensky. 1993. Optimality theory: Constraint interaction in generative grammar. ms.

Jason Alan Riggle. 2004. *Generation, recognition, and learning in finite state Optimality Theory*. Ph.D. thesis, Citeseer.

Bounded-Depth High-Coverage Search Space for Noncrossing Parses

Anssi Yli-Jyrä
University of Helsinki, Finland
`anssi.yli-jyra@helsinki.fi`

Abstract

A recently proposed encoding for non-crossing digraphs can be used to implement generic inference over families of these digraphs and to carry out first-order factored dependency parsing. It is now shown that the recent proposal can be substantially streamlined without information loss. The improved encoding is less dependent on hierarchical processing and it gives rise to a *high-coverage bounded-depth approximation* of the space of noncrossing digraphs. This subset is presented elegantly by a *finite-state machine* that recognizes an infinite set of encoded graphs. The set includes more than 99.99% of the 0.6 million noncrossing graphs obtained from the UDv2 treebanks through planarisation. Rather than taking the low probability of the residual as a flat rate, it can be modelled with a joint probability distribution that is factorised into two underlying stochastic processes – the *sentence length distribution* and the related *conditional distribution for deep nesting*. This model points out that deep nesting in the streamlined code requires extreme sentence lengths. High depth is categorically out in common sentence lengths but emerges slowly at infrequent lengths that prompt further inquiry.

Syntactic and semantic dependency structures – rooted trees and more general digraphs – have tremendous importance in multilingual language analysis as demonstrated by the Universal Dependencies (UD) initiative[1] and many applications of dependency annotations. The main approaches

to produce dependency structures include *graph-based parsers* (Eisner and Satta, 1999; McDonald et al., 2005) that build the structures in the bottom up fashion and *transition-based parsers* that produce structures while reading the input buffer (Nivre, 2008; Bohnet et al., 2016).

Recently, Yli-Jyrä and Gómez-Rodríguez (2017) have explored a perspective that combines graph-based parsing with coding theory: instead of rewriting digraphs directly, they propose a linear encoding for noncrossing digraphs and then manipulate the code strings using string automata. This method brings the two parsing approaches closer to each other as the graphical parsing reduces to a combination of state-driven processing of the underlying regular component and graphical processing of context-free component of the encoding. Their main result is that some 50 natural families of dependency structures reduce to unambiguous context-free languages. Generic parsing to noncrossing digraphs can thus be viewed as weighted context-free parsing.

The parsing objective in the framework of Yli-Jyrä and Gómez-Rodríguez (2017) is to maximize the total arc weight of the parse using an exact cubic-time inference procedure over the language associated with the input sentence. Polynomial time is often too expensive as such alternative methods as transition-based parsing with beam search may produce similar accuracy in linear time. Since higher efficiency is welcome in many real-time data applications, one may ask whether the encoded search space could be optimized to allow efficient, linear-time inference over *the most plausible* candidate graphs.

In this paper, we present an improved representation for the search space. First, the linear encoding of noncrossing graphs is streamlined by a technique called *weak edge bracketing*. Second, the context-free language of the streamlined en-

---

[1] `http://universaldependencies.org/`

Proceedings of the 13th International Conference on Finite State Methods and Natural Language Processing, pages 30–40,
Umeå, Sweden, 4–6 September 2017. © 2017 Association for Computational Linguistics
https://doi.org/10.18653/v1/W17-4004

coding is further *approximated* with a regular subset that contains the most probable dependency analyses. This gives us a finite-state representation of the search space. We also construct a *factored joint probability model* for the event that the correct parse is outside of the search space. Under the approximation and the current experiments, the probability for a failure is less than 0.3% for all languages and 0.006% on average.

The low error rate means that if the proposed approximation was used to restrict the search space of the state-of-the-art parsers, the obtained finite-state approximation would potentially improve the efficiency significantly while leaving the parsing accuracy nearly intact. When used in this way as a search space restriction, the currently proposed regular approximations for the families of digraphs – as proposed by Yli-Jyrä and Gómez-Rodríguez (2017) – become available to higher-order graphical parsers, neural transition-based parsers and generative neural models of syntax.

The current paper focuses on the structure and the motivation for the finite-state search space for noncrossing digraphs. Section 2 presents the problem of finding a good finite-state approximation of the search space. The streamlined context-free encoding for the noncrossing digraphs is introduced in Section 3. Sections 4 and 5 discuss its minimum-DFA state complexity and coverage under a bounded nesting depth. Before conclusion, the results are related to the prior work and discussed critically in Section 6.

1 Definitions

In this section, I follow Yli-Jyrä and Gómez-Rodríguez (2017) to define noncrossing dependency graphs and describe how they can be encoded as linear strings.

Graphs A *graph* is a pair (V,E) where V is a finite set of vertices and $E \subseteq \{\{u,v\} \subseteq V\}$ is a set of edges. It is common to assume that the edges do not contain self-loops of the form $\{v,v\}$. For convenience, the vertices in graphs are ordered $V = [1,...,n]$. Two edges $\{i,j\}$, $\{k,l\}$ in an ordered graph are said to be *crossing* if $\min\{i,j\} < \min\{k,l\} < \max\{i,j\} < \max\{k,l\}$. A graph is *noncrossing* if it has no crossing edges.

Yli-Jyrä and Gómez-Rodríguez (2017) have proposed a scheme according to which any noncrossing ordered graph $([1,...,n],E)$ is encoded as a string of brackets using the algorithm `enc` in

```
func enc(n,E):                func dec(stdin):
  for i in [1,...,n]:           n = 1; E = {}; s = []
    for j in [i-1,...,2,1]:     while c in stdin:
      if {j,i} in E:              if c == "[":
        print "]"                    s.push(n)
    for j in [n,n-1,...,i+1]:     if c == "]":
      if {i,j} in E:                 i = s.pop()
        print "["                    E.insert((i,n))
    if i<n:                        if c == "{":
      print "{}"                      n = n + 1
                                return (n,E)
```

Figure 1: The encoding and decoding algorithms

Fig. 1. For example, the output for the ordered graph

$$n = 4, \quad E = \left\{ \begin{array}{ll} \{1,2\}, & \\ \{2,4\}, & \{1,4\} \end{array} \right\}$$

is the string `[[{}][{}{}]]`. Intuitively, pairs of brackets of the form {} can be interpreted as spaces between vertices, and then each set of matching brackets `[...]` encodes an arc that covers the spaces represented inside the brackets.

The noncrossing ordered graphs are encoded with strings that constitute a context-free language. These *encoded graphs* are generated exactly by the context-free grammar $S \to [S'] \, S \mid \{\} \, S \mid \varepsilon, \; S' \to [S'] \, T \mid \{\} \, S, \, T \to [S'] \, S \mid \{\} \, S$. This language of encoded graph corresponds bijectively to the set of all non-crossing graphs.

Digraphs The encoding scheme extends to digraphs. A *digraph* is a pair (V,A) where $A \subseteq V \times V$ is a set of arcs $u \to v$. Its *underlying graph*, (V,E_A), has edges $E_A = \{\{u,v\} \mid (u,v) \in A\}$. A *noncrossing digraph* is a digraph whose underlying graph is noncrossing. Any noncrossing ordered digraph $([1,...,n],A)$ can be encoded with slight modifications to the encoding algorithm. Instead of printing `[ ]` for an edge $\{i,j\} \in E_A, i \leq j$, the algorithm should now print

$$
\begin{array}{ll}
/ \;\; > & \text{if } (i,j) \in A, (j,i) \notin A; \\
< \;\; \backslash & \text{if } (i,j) \notin A, (j,i) \in A; \\
[\;\;] & \text{if } (i,j), (j,i) \in A.
\end{array}
$$

In this way, we can simply encode the digraph $(\{1,2,3,4\},\{(1,2),(4,1),(4,2)\})$ as the string `</{}><{}{}\\`. Again, there is a bijection between noncrossing digraphs and their encodings, L_{DIGRAPHS}. All n-vertex noncrossing digraphs are represented with the language

$$L_{\text{DIGRAPHS}} \cap W^n \qquad (1)$$

where $W^n = \overline{B}^* (\{\}\overline{B}^*)^{n-1}$ describes the alternation between vertex boundaries {} and edge brackets $\overline{B}$ that exclude these boundaries.

Yli-Jyrä and Gómez-Rodríguez (2017) construct representations of context-free languages that encode important families of digraphs and graphs. Accordingly, there are context-free languages that correspond to the rooted noncrossing trees, projective trees, noncrossing dags etc.

Dependency Parsing The *complete digraph* (V,A) *of a sentence* $S = x_1 \ldots x_n$ consists of vertices $V = \{1, \ldots, n\}$ and all possible arcs $A = \{(i,j) \mid i \neq j\}$. In the *arc-factored* model (McDonald et al., 2005), every arc $i \to j$ in this digraph is equipped with a positive weight w_{ij} that is predicted on the basis of the feature vectors associated with tokens i and j in the sentence. To facilitate local weight assignment to the pairs of brackets in the encoding, the brackets in the encoded digraphs (1) can be indexed with the corresponding vertex numbers. This indexing turns string $[[\{\}][\{\}\{\}]]$ into $[_1[_1\{\}]_2[_2\{\}\{\}]_4]_4$. The total weight of this string is computed using a dynamically constructed semiring-weighted context-free grammar

$$S \to \varepsilon \mid \{\};$$

$$S \overset{w_{12}}{\to} [_1S]_2S; \quad S \overset{w_{13}}{\to} [_1S]_3S; \quad S \overset{w_{14}}{\to} [_1S]_4S;$$

$$S \overset{w_{23}}{\to} [_2S]_3S; \quad S \overset{w_{24}}{\to} [_2S]_4S; \quad S \overset{w_{34}}{\to} [_3S]_4S.$$

Let $\otimes$ be a commutative monoid operation used to compute the total weight of a derivation under the grammar. For the above string, the grammar then returns the total weight $w_{12} \otimes w_{24} \otimes w_{14}$.

The task of *arc-factored dependency parsing* is to find in the specified family of the graphs (e.g. noncrossing dags), the maximal subgraph (V,A') of the complete digraph (V,A). When the inference is restricted to a noncrossing family L_{FAMILY} of digraphs, the natural choice is to carry out the inference using a cubic-time algorithm that recognises the weighted context-free language and finds the indexed string $w \in L_{\text{FAMILY}} \cap W_n$ that maximizes the total weight of the derivation.

2 The Problem

For long sentences, a linear-time parsing algorithm can be considerably more efficient and attractive than a cubic-time parsing algorithm. Since the encoded digraphs support generic parsing to different families of digraphs, we would now like to provide foundations for a linear time variant of this generic parsing architecture. The most obvious approach would be to replace the context-free

grammar of (di)graphs with a regular subset approximation.

Since the approximation is regular, there are at most a finite number of equivalence classes over possible parser states at any moment. The number of equivalence classes tells the size of a deterministic finite automaton. The search space of an arbitrary sentence consists of those digraphs that are encoded by the intersection of the language L'_{FAMILY} recognized by this automaton and the language W_n defining the position-indexed brackets.

A good, practical approximation must satisfy at least three requirements:

- **Complete core**. A language-independent and generic approximation for the set of digraphs should certainly contain all digraphs over a small number ($n \leq 7$) of tokens.

- **Convenient size**. The amount of the memory needed to carry out inference over long sentences should not stretch the limits of a convenient implementation.

- **Good coverage**. The approximation should have a good coverage of the existing analyses in treebanks.

During the inference for the best parse, the memory of a typical algorithm stores the parse candidates either as a non-center-embedding grammar or a fully expanded finite-state automaton that represents the crossproduct of two finite-state representations, one for the search space and one for the strings with vertex indexed bracket. Since the convenience of the expanded representation is not at all obvious, the current work focuses on its deterministic state complexity, i.e. the number of states in a minimal DFAs recognizer.

With the encoding scheme of Yli-Jyrä and Gómez-Rodríguez (2017), the state complexity of the DFA-based search space representation grows rapidly when the length of the sentence increases. This comes from the fact that the states must keep track of four kinds of open brackets: [, <, /, {.

n	encoded digraphs	states
1	1	1
2	4	12
3	64	80
4	1 792	490
5	62 464	2 952
6	2 437 120	27 040
7	101 859 328	106 372

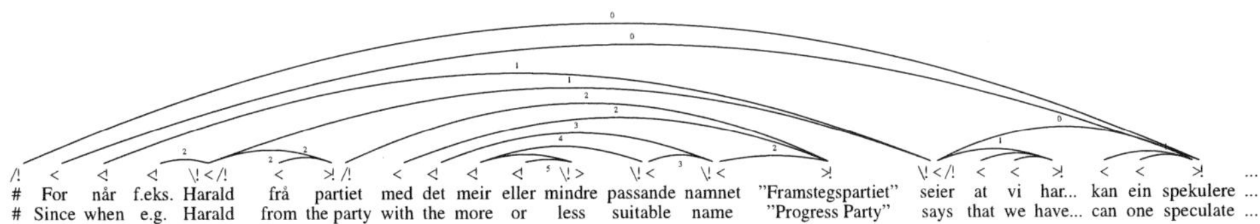

Figure 2: An example of a parse tree that requires weak bracketing with nesting depth 5.

By the **Complete core** requirement, we obtain a rough lower-bound state complexity for the required approximation L'_{FAMILY}. The search space for $n = 7$ equals to the intersection $W_{n=7} \cap L'_{\text{FAMILY}}$ whose state complexity is $106\,372$ states. Since the recognizer for W_7 requires exactly 14 states, the recognizer G for L'_{FAMILY} should contain at least $\lceil 106\,372/14 \rceil = 7\,598$ states as the cross product of these automata cannot have fewer than $106\,372$ states. With this $7\,598$-state automaton G, the parsing of a 500-token sentence would require at least $|W_{500}||G| = 7\,598\,000$ states.[2] But an automaton of this size is usually inconvenient to operate with and does not satisfy the **Convenient size** requirement.[3] Since only 6 overlapping edges are observed in 7-word sentences, this approximation would also fail to cover treebanks where more than 10 nested edges are quite common (Figure 2), breaking the **Good coverage** requirement. Thus, a DFA approximation based on the prior encoding is doomed to fail in the real life scenario.[4]

The current research problem is to improve the representation of the search space in such a way that fewer DFA states are needed and more complex structures can be captured with a convenient number of equivalence classes.

3 The Improved Encoding

The prior encoding can be improved through weak, reduced bracketing that packs adjacent closing or opening brackets into a single symbol. The idea has historical links to superbrackets in Interlisp (Teitelman, 1978), but similar ideas have been introduced to the bracketing of phrase struc-

ture trees (Langendoen, 1975; Krauwer and des Tombe, 1981; Yli-Jyrä, 2003). In the context of edge brackets, the idea of weak bracketing appears partially in Yli-Jyrä (2004).

3.1 Nested Sibling Edges

The key observation is that nested sibling edges give rise to adjacent copies of one-sided brackets:

$$\underbrace{[\ [\ [\ [\ [}_{\text{similar}}\ \{\}\ ]\ \{\}\ ]\ \{\}\ ]\ \{\}\ ]\ \{\}\ ]$$

The idea is that if we indicate both sides of the outermost sibling edge, its nested siblings share one of its ends and thus need only a one-sided bracket:

$$\underbrace{[\,!}_{\text{shareable}}\ \{\}\ ]\ \{\}\ ]\ \{\}\ ]\ \{\}\ ]\ \{\}\ \underbrace{]\,!}_{\text{shareable}}$$

Our current contribution to this idea is to observe that (1) both sides of the outermost brackets can be shared and (2) that every edge can be independently directed or undirected:

$$\underbrace{[\ \ [\ /\ \{\}\ >\ \{\}\ ]\ \{\}\ <\ \{\}\ /\ \{\}\ >\ \backslash\ ]}$$
$$[\,!\quad \{\}\ >\ \{\}\ ]\ \{\}\ <\ \{\}\ /\ \{\}\quad]\,!$$

Figure 2 shows how this encoding is applied to a real dependency tree.

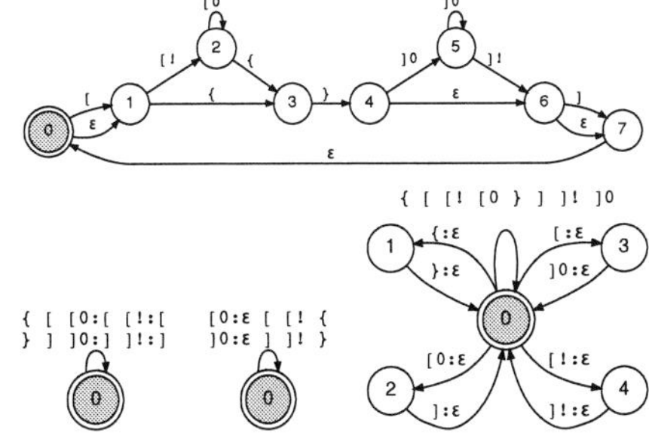

Figure 3: Language C and functions Y and E and relation T_4

---

[2] The seven longest sentences in the UDv2 dataset viewed by the author consist of 399, 428, 493, 496, 504, 534 and 610 tokens.

[3] A hierarchical grammar representation would be much more succinct but it assumes richer structures that we would like to preserve for optimizations of the implementation.

[4] We did not even consider the latent encoding of Yli-Jyrä and Gómez-Rodríguez. The latent encoding has a more complex local structure and requires drastically more states in a DFA representation.

3.2 Re-encoder

There is a transducer that converts the original
"strong" edge bracketing into weak edge bracketing. The transducer is represented with four components in Figure 3:

1. Sequential function Y that replaces the *super
   brackets*]!, [!, the *redundant brackets*]0,
   [0 and the *weak brackets*], [with standard
   edge brackets], [, respectively.

2. Language C that states the property that weak
   brackets], [are not appearing at the position
   of redundant brackets and that the redundant
   brackets]0, [0 are attached locally to a similar super bracket]!, [!.

3. Sequential function E that elides the redundant brackets.

4. A reflexive regular relation T_4 whose iterated
   application implements the fact that balanced
   brackets may cancel each other.

If X is a finite set of encoded graphs, we can
re-encode these graphs as the corresponding set of
weakly bracketed graphs X_w. We compute

$$X_w = \mathbf{Dom}(E^{-1} \circ \underbrace{\mathbf{Dom}(Y \circ X) \circ C \circ T_4 \circ ... \circ T_4 \circ \varepsilon)}_{... \circ T_4 \circ T_4 \text{ until fixed point}}$$

where **Dom** returns the input projection and X, C
and ε are viewed as identity relations. Since the
composition closure $T_4 \circ T_4 \circ ... \circ T_4 \circ \varepsilon$ maps the
balanced bracket strings to the empty word, its in-
put projection is actually a Dyck language D_4 — a
balanced language over the four kinds of balanced
brackets. With this context-free language, we can
define the re-encoder as function

$$X_w = E(Y^{-1}(X) \cap C \cap D_4).$$

that maps the strongly bracketed strings X to the
weakly bracketed strings X_w. This re-encoder
function extends to encoded digraphs in the natural way by extending the set of brackets.

3.3 Improved State Complexity

The state complexity of the set of all n-vertex noncrossing digraphs for the streamlined encoding is
essentially smaller than previously:

n	encoded digraphs	states
...		
5	62 464	207
6	2 437 120	704
7	101 859 328	1327

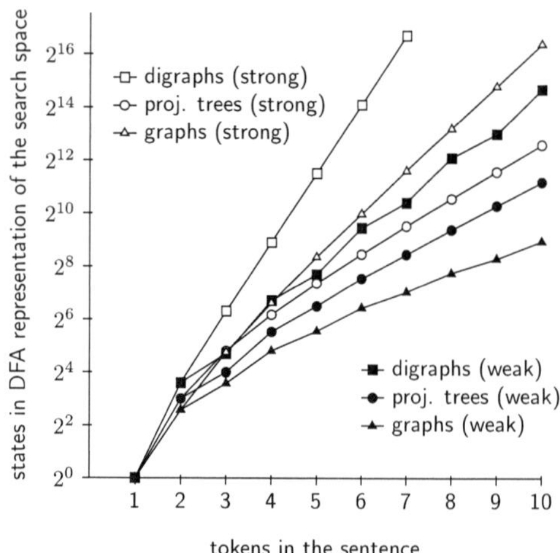

Figure 4: Weak bracketing brings exponential savings in the size of the DFA representing the search
space of a sentence when the search space consists
of digraphs, projective trees, or graphs

We are also able to go beyond $n = 7$ and build
complete search spaces of undirected graphs with
more vertices:

n	encoded graphs	states
10	21 292 032	490
19	29 312 424 612 462 592	12 395
20	314 739 971 287 154 688	18 276
21	3 393 951 437 605 044 224	24 925
30	$\approx 7.681 \cdot 10^{27}$	589 598

Figure 4 shows that the state complexity difference between the original and the new encoding
scheme for digraphs, projective trees and graphs
is indeed exponential to the length of the sentences. With the simple trick that replaces / ! and
< ! with [!, but otherwise separates the brack-
ets /, >,], [, <, \, [!,]!, \!, >!, the
search space generalizes from noncrossing graphs
to noncrossing digraphs *without any increase in
the state complexity*. This gives another significant
saving in the state complexity of digraph search
space compared to the original encoding.[5]

3.4 The Context-Free Set of Digraphs

There is an extended context-free grammar that
generates all encoded undirected graphs using the

---

[5]Some further savings could be obtained by joining the
adjacent curly brackets { } into an atomic symbol.

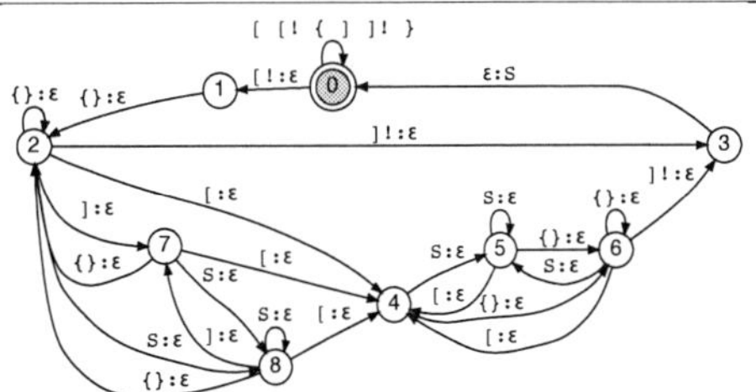

$$S' \to (\{\} \mid S)^*$$
$$S \to \;[!\left(\{\} \mid T(\{\} \mid S)^* U\right)]! \text{ where}$$
$$T = \{\} \mid \{\}(\{\} \mid S)^*] \left((\{\} \mid S)^+]\right)^*$$
$$U = \{\} \mid \left([(\{\} \mid S)^+\right)^* [(\{\} \mid S)^* \{\}$$

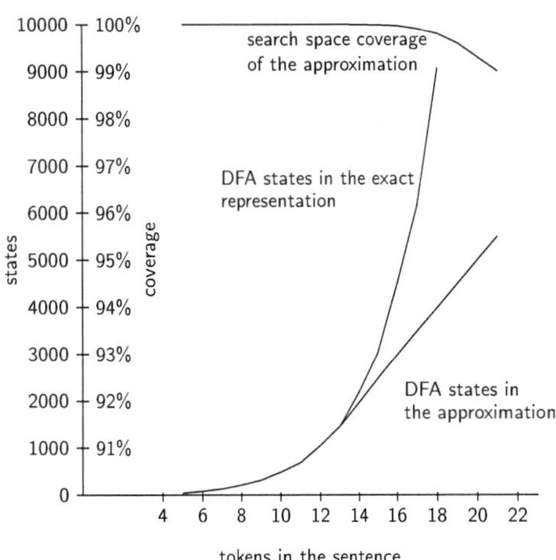

Figure 5: Top left: the level grammar. Top right: a bottom-up recognizer G_S for S.

weak edge bracketing:

$$S' \to S^* \tag{2}$$
$$S \to \{\} \mid [!\{\}]! \mid [!\,T S^* U\,]! \tag{3}$$
$$T \to \{\} \mid \{\}S^*] \left(SS^*]\right)^* \tag{4}$$
$$U \to \{\} \mid \left([SS^*\right)^* [S^*\{\} \tag{5}$$

The derivation steps of this grammar do not correspond exactly to nesting of brackets. The grammar can, however, be converted to an extended context-free grammar where each derivation step corresponds to a new nesting level. This is illustrated in the left of Figure 5.

We implement the grammar as a transducer that is iterated until the sentential form is in the language $(\{\} \mid S)^*$. The iterated transducer G_S is shown in the right of Figure 5.

4 Finite-State Search Space

A finite-state approximation is obtained from the grammar by composing copies of the bottom-up recognizer G_S and by restricting the output language to $(\{\} \mid S)^*$. The language $L'_{\text{GRAPHS}(5)}$ is constructed using 6 copies of the G_S transducer:

$$\mathbf{Dom}(G_S \circ G_S \circ G_S \circ G_S \circ G_S \circ G_S \circ (\{\} \mid S)^*)$$

The language $L'_{\text{GRAPHS}(5)}$ has 442 distinguishable DFA states and 1388 transitions. This approximation of the grammar can be used to represent most of the search space of n-vertex sentences with fewer states than the length-limited finite subset of context-free language L_{GRAPHS} that contains all graphs. When $L'_{\text{GRAPHS}(5)}$ and L_{GRAPHS} are constrained with W_n, we obtain regular languages whose state complexity can be measured. The difference between these is illustrated in Figure 6.

It is interesting that although the approximation captures only 6 levels (5 nested ones) of super brackets, it gives exact results until the graphs

Figure 6: In terms of space complexity, the approximation grows only linearly to the sentence length while the exact search space representation explodes quickly. Meanwhile, the finite nesting depth has only a slowly growing proportional effect on the the search space when the length of the sentence increases.

have 14 vertices. This is because each pair of superbrackets encode an edge whose two endpoints are non-incident with the edges that correspond to nested superbrackets.

Since the approximated search space grows linearly to the sentence length, the approximated search space of 21-vertex graphs requires 5 501 states. Interestingly, this subset approximation still covers 99% of the complete search space as it contains 3 358 682 892 406 358 016 graphs.

5 Data Coverage

The length of real sentences in treebanks and in texts varies a lot. At very high lengths, it is not easy to tell without real data how probable it is

Table 1: The coverage of UD v.2 data with depth bounded weak edge bracketing

lang	N	depth 0	depth 1	depth 2	depth 3	depth 4	depth 5	depth 6	depth 7
Arabic	26722	4.42%	20.93%	65.09%	94.39%	99.64%	99.99%	+0.011% (3)	
Catalan	14832	1.27%	19.01%	70.39%	96.07%	99.62%	99.99%	+0.007% (1)	
Czech	102660	10.60%	43.11%	86.77%	98.47%	99.89%	99.99%	+0.010% (10)	
German	14917	2.06%	43.11%	87.52%	98.56%	99.91%	99.97%	+0.027% (4)	
English	19785	16.61%	53.59%	91.10%	99.21%	99.96%	100.00%		
Spanish	31546	1.59%	24.61%	77.27%	97.24%	99.79%	100.00%	+0.003% (1)	
Finnish	30437	30.03%	77.46%	96.54%	99.55%	99.96%	99.99%	+0.007% (2)	
French	19294	2.86%	37.87%	88.24%	98.89%	99.94%	99.99%	+0.005% (1)	
Greek	28478	16.47%	67.77%	95.75%	99.73%	99.98%	100.00%		
Hebrew	5725	1.61%	24.63%	80.61%	98.72%	99.93%	100.00%		
Hindi	14963	0.45%	37.19%	82.74%	98.04%	99.90%	99.98%	+0.020% (3)	
Croatian	8289	2.23%	33.78%	86.39%	98.90%	99.93%	100.00%		
Hungarian	1351	1.11%	22.95%	68.91%	94.89%	98.96%	99.78%	+0.148% (2)	+0.074% (1)
Italian	14992	4.93%	47.62%	88.22%	98.63%	99.92%	100.00%		
Japanese	7675	1.98%	48.60%	96.73%	99.96%	100.00%	100.00%		
Latin	33166	20.14%	61.14%	90.57%	98.86%	99.94%	100.00%		
Latvian	3054	16.50%	57.50%	88.93%	98.23%	99.80%	99.97%		+0.033% (1)
Dutch	19891	18.32%	60.86%	93.81%	99.56%	99.98%	100.00%		
Polish	7127	13.03%	75.28%	98.58%	99.94%	99.99%	100.00%		
Portuguese	19765	4.61%	32.02%	81.33%	97.98%	99.83%	99.99%	+0.005% (1)	
Romanian	8795	0.80%	25.78%	84.51%	98.53%	99.87%	99.99%	+0.011% (1)	
Russian	59827	12.57%	73.86%	97.03%	99.76%	99.98%	100.00%	+0.002% (1)	
Slovenian	9349	17.82%	57.60%	94.34%	99.68%	99.99%	100.00%		
Scandinavian	47574	12.46%	55.27%	92.52%	99.35%	99.96%	100.00%		
Turkish	4660	22.08%	71.20%	92.68%	98.88%	99.89%	99.98%	+ 0.021% (1)	
Chinese	4497	0.00%	19.64%	70.49%	94.53%	99.51%	99.96%	+ 0.044% (2)	
other UD treebanks	71147	12.55%	57.43%	91.58%	99.21%	99.96%	100.00%		
	630518	11.07%	50.38%	88.38%	98.66%	99.91%	99.994%	+ 0.005% (33)	+ 0.0003% (2)

that a finite-state approximation does not contain the correct analysis graph or digraph. In order to learn about the probability of the out-of-the-search-space event, we used the UD treebanks as the first proxy to find out how often a given nesting depth is exceeded in gold trees.

Our current encoding can handle only noncrossing trees such as projective trees. However, the trees in UD version 2 treebanks do not have this restriction. It is well known that the proportion of non-projective, and thus crossing, trees is relatively high for some languages (Gómez-Rodríguez, 2016). If all nonprojective analyses were discarded, most of the long sentences would have been excluded, with significant effect on our experiments.

For the experiments, we had to enforce non-crossing structure to the data. The standard approach is to perform lift transformations that move crossing edges higher in the dependency tree. Although there are methods to minimize the number of lifts either heuristically or exactly, the output of such a transformation is not uniquely determined. The second way to projectivise trees is to keep the dominance tree intact but reorder the nodes of the tree into a canonical order that maintains the relative order of the immediate dependents of each head. The third approach, actually used by us, views the trees as undirected trees and takes advantage of the algebraic properties of bal-

anced bracketing. For example, if we combine the edge brackets in [{}{}][{}] and {}[{}{}], we obtain [{}[{}][{}]] that encodes a slightly different set of edges. This method works also with reduced bracketing where the opening and closing superbrackets cancel one another. The resulting code string preserves the number of edges but some ends of these edges may change. The result may be a cyclic or disconnected graph but it preserves noncrossing parts of the graph intact because there the brackets match the two ends of each edge.

The total number of sentences in the sample was 630 518. This includes both the training and the development sections of the UD v.2 treebanks. The data was encoded with our new encoding scheme and automatically converted to noncrossing undirected graphs before the nesting depth of each sentence was computed.[6]

Table 1 describes how the nesting depth corresponds to coverage in the UD2 data set. It indicates that the depth 5 is a good compromise between depth and coverage. Under this depth, the search space contains 99.994% of all the trees in the treebanks. Only 35 sentences require weak bracketing whose nesting depth is more than 5. Thus the flat out-of-the-search-space failure rate is 0.006% of the sentences only.

---

[6]The code for the encoding script is in `https://github.com/amikael/depconv`.

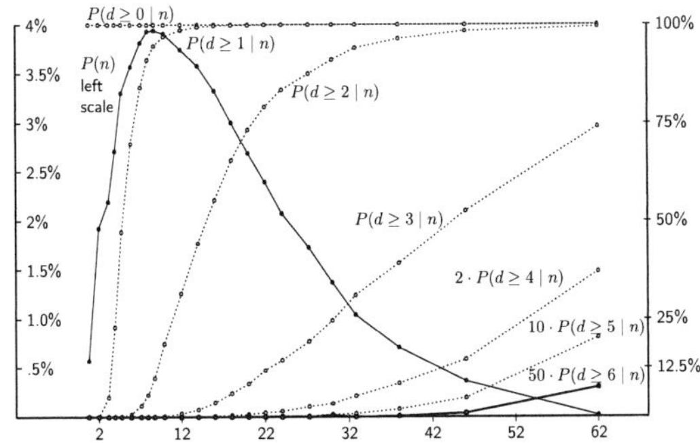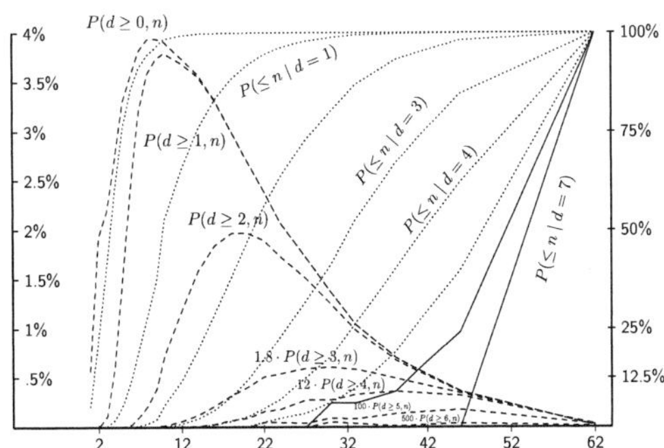

Figure 7: Left: the sentence length distribution $P(n\text{-bucket}) = \text{count}(n-\text{bucket})/\text{all sentences}$ and the conditional probability $P(d \geq k \mid n) = \text{count}(d, n-\text{bucket})/\text{count}(n-\text{bucket})$ of exceeding depth of weak bracketing, given the sentence length. Right: the joint distribution $P(d \geq k \mid n\text{-bucket}) = \text{count}(d, n-\text{bucket})/\text{bucketsize/total}$ for the event of exceeding depth, given sentence length and the conditional distribution $P(\leq n \mid d) = \text{count}(\leq n-\text{bucket}, d)/\text{count}(d)$ of maximum sentence length, given the bracketing depth. Scaling of some distributions was necessary as the numeric values of some nearby distributions are of different orders of magnitude.

The error rate leaves us with doubts about the representativeness of the sample. To gain more insight into the underlying process, a more sophisticated statistical model was constructed. For this purpose, the multilingual data was smoothed by splitting the sentence lengths into buckets that contained typically some 30k sentences. The length ranges were $[2,2], ..., [9,9], [10,11], ..., [24,25], [26,28], [29,31], [32,35], [36,41], [42,52], [53,610]$. Each was represented by the length of the median sentence in the range. E.g. the range $[53,610]$ was represented by the median length 62.

The sentence length and nesting depth combine to form a joint distribution $P(d > k, n)$ that can be factored in different ways. Figure 7 presents the distribution of sentence lengths and the related conditional and joint distributions as they could be observed. The statistics reveal the following observations:

1. The shape of the sentence length distribution resembles a Poisson distribution.[7]

2. Although the sentence length increases, the probability of shallow bracketing still remains high (e.g. $P(d < 4 \mid n \in [42,52]) = 0.93\%$), as the probability of a deep nesting event increases slowly according to the sentence length.

3. The observed probability of a deep sentence grows almost linearly when the sentence length increases. Thus, high sentence length does not necessarily mean very deep nesting ($P(d \geq 6 \mid n \in [42,610]) < 0.2\%$). Even extremely long sentences are rarely deep ($P(d \geq 6 \mid n \in [53,610]) = 0.15\%$).

4. The current experiments seem to break the direct link from long sentences to deep nesting but supports the opposite tendency. The probability of a sentence being deep is zero when the number of tokens is less than 14, but very deep nesting predicts high sentence length ($P(n > 45 \mid d = 6) > 99\%$).

5. The proportion of deep analyses in the search space is higher than the corresponding proportion in the real data for each length. In particular, deep nesting in sentences with 20-21 tokens is expected to happen almost at the probability 1% if all analyses were equally probable (Figure 6), but observed probability of the event is under 0.002% ($P(d \geq 6 \mid n \in [20,21]) = 0.002\%$).

6 Discussion

There are three factors that contribute to deep nesting structures in bracketed binarised trees:

- **Tail Recursion.** Repeated left- and right-branching structures generate initial and final forms of tail recursion, as well as zigzag embedding that involves both.

---

[7] For a sophisticated sentence length model, see e.g. Sichel (1974).

- **Unit Rules**. Non-branching trees embed trees in a way that may generate new nesting levels in bracketing.

- **Local Factorization**. Local factorization of unranked parse trees and unbounded sibling edges can generate unbounded recursion.

Unit rules and tail recursion have been addressed in several prior studies as their naive bracketing may involve unbounded stack or nested brackets. The prior approaches include grammar transformations in parsers (Langendoen, 1975; Johnson, 1998; Nederhof, 2000), weak bracketing of constituent trees (Langendoen and Langsam, 1984; Krauwer and des Tombe, 1981; Black, 1989; Koskenniemi, 1990; Yli-Jyrä, 2003), edge bracketing of dependency trees (Oflazer, 2003; Yli-Jyrä, 2005, 2012; Yli-Jyrä et al., 2012) and further ideas (Church, 1980; Langendoen, 2008; Hulden and Silfverberg, 2014).

The current work goes another mile in the study of bounded nesting by introducing weak edge bracketing that avoids unbounded recursion when unbounded local trees are binarized and bracketed.[8] The work also shows that the classic technique can be extended to all noncrossing digraphs. This extends the relevance of finite-state transducer techniques from syntax to semantic dependency parsing.

The weak edge bracketing is effective in improving the state complexity of finite sets of noncrossing digraphs (Figure 4). Thanks to the new bracketing scheme, the coverage of depth-bounded approximations is very high and seems to deteriorate slower than the state complexity of the exact search space grows (Figure 6). A further improvement was obtained by the trick that maintained the state complexity when the encoding for graphs was generalized to digraphs.

A careful comparison between methods that ensure noncrossing structures could reveal some interesting differences. While the nonprojective trees can be projectivised (and thus turned into noncrossing graphs) with optimal number of lifts, the lifted tree is still not unique and it may be intractable to optimize the nesting depth over the choices. It may also be a problem if the input is not a tree and therefore the existing graph banks should be also explored in the statistics.

Natural next steps in the proposed methodology would be to adapt the parametrizable parsing framework of Yli-Jyrä and Gómez-Rodríguez (2017) to weak bracketing and to implement a linear-time arc-factored parser to important families of non-crossing digraphs. It is also important to find ways to combine the current encoding with higher-order dependency parsing and neural network grammars that weight local trees. The main challenge is, however, to extend the current work to crossing graphs and nonprojective trees.

7 Conclusion

In this paper, we have presented the first weak edge bracketing scheme for noncrossing digraphs and described the bijectively related context-free language of code strings. Our scheme improves over (Yli-Jyrä and Gómez-Rodríguez, 2017) as the minimum DFA state complexity of search space representations is smaller and unranked dependencies can be processed without recursion.

The experiments indicate that 5 nested levels of balanced brackets are sufficient to cover nearly all noncrossing UD v.2 data. According the joint distribution of length and depth, deep nesting is a rare event that correlates with an exceptional sentence length.

The language $L'_{\text{GRAPHS}(5)}$ representing the subset approximation of the search space for all noncrossing graphs with nesting depth 5 can be applied beyond the Yli-Jyrä and Gómez-Rodríguez (2017) framework to guide and restrict syntactic parsing and generation. This is expected to lead to linear time syntactic and semantic dependency parsing with noncrossing output structures. If combined with multiplanar/book embedding methods (Yli-Jyrä, 2003; Kuhlmann and Johnsson, 2015), the techniques might extend to non-projective parsing and crossing graphs.

Acknowledgements

The author has received funding as Research Fellow from the Academy of Finland (dec. No 270354 - A Usable Finite-State Model for Adequate Syntactic Complexity) and Clare Hall Fellow from the University of Helsinki (dec. RP 137/2013 - SMT based on D-Tree Contraction Grammars and FSTs). He is indebted to Kimmo Koskenniemi, Jussi Piitulainen, Carlos Gómez-Rodríguez and the anonymous reviewers for helpful comments on earlier stages of the research.

---

[8]The idea started to develop already in Yli-Jyrä (2004).

References

Alan W. Black. 1989. Finite state machines from feature grammars. In Masaru Tomita, editor, *International Workshop on Parsing Technologies*, Carnegie Mellon Univeristy Press, Pittsburgh, Pennsylvania, pages 277–285.

Bernd Bohnet, Emily Pitler, Ji Ma, and Ryan Mcdonald. 2016. Generalized transition-based dependency parsing. In *Association for Computational Linguistics (ACL)*. https://www.aclweb.org/anthology/P16-1015.

Kenneth Church. 1980. On parsing strategies and closure. In *18th ACL 1980, Proceedings of the Conference*. Philadelphia, Pennsylvania, USA, pages 107–111. http://www.aclweb.org/anthology/P80-1028.

Jason Eisner and Giorgio Satta. 1999. Efficient parsing for bilexical context-free grammars and Head Automaton Grammars. In *Proceedings of the 37th Annual Meeting of the Association for Computational Linguistics*. Association for Computational Linguistics, College Park, Maryland, USA, pages 457–464. https://doi.org/10.3115/1034678.1034748.

Carlos Gómez-Rodríguez. 2016. Restricted non-projectivity: Coverage vs. efficiency. *Computational Linguistics* 42(4):809–817. https://doi.org/10.1162/COLI_a_00267.

Mans Hulden and Miikka Silfverberg. 2014. Finite-state subset approximation of phrase structure. In *International Symposium on Artificial Intelligence and Mathematics*. Fort Lauderdale, USA.

Mark Johnson. 1998. Finite-state approximation of constraint-based grammars using left-corner grammar transforms. In *36th ACL 1998, 17th COLING 1998, Proceedings of the Conference*. Montréal, Quebec, Canada, volume 1, pages 619–623. http://aclweb.org/anthology/P/P98/P98-1101.pdf.

Kimmo Koskenniemi. 1990. Finite-state parsing and disambiguation. In Hans Karlgren, editor, *13th COLING 1990, Proceedings of the Conference*. Helsinki, Finland, volume 2, pages 229–232. https://doi.org/0.3115/997939.997979.

Steven Krauwer and Louis des Tombe. 1981. Transducers and grammars as theories of language. *Theoretical Linguistics* 8:173–202. https://doi.org/10.1515/thli.1981.8.1-3.173.

Marco Kuhlmann and Peter Johnsson. 2015. Parsing to noncrossing dependency graphs. *Transactions of the Association for Computational Linguistics* 3:559–570. http://aclweb.org/anthology/Q/Q15/Q15-1040.pdf.

D. Terence Langendoen. 1975. Finite-state parsing of phrase-structure languages and the status of readjustment rules in grammar. *Linguistic Inquiry* VI(4):533–554. http://www.jstor.org/stable/4177899.

D. Terence Langendoen. 2008. Coordinate grammar. *Language* 84(4):691–709. http://www.jstor.org/stable/40071100.

D. Terence Langendoen and Yedidyah Langsam. 1984. The representation of constituent structures for finite-state parsing. In *22th ACL 1984, 10th COLING 1984, Proceedings of the Conference*. Stanford, CA, USA, pages 24–27. http://www.aclweb.org/anthology/P84-1007.

Ryan McDonald, Fernando Pereira, Kiril Ribarov, and Jan Hajic. 2005. Non-projective dependency parsing using spanning tree algorithms. In *Proceedings of Human Language Technology Conference and Conference on Empirical Methods in Natural Language Processing*. Association for Computational Linguistics, Vancouver, British Columbia, Canada, pages 523–530. http://www.aclweb.org/anthology/H/H05/H05-1066.pdf.

Mark-Jan Nederhof. 2000. Practical experiments with regular approximation of context-free languages. *Computational Linguistics* 26(1):17–44. https://doi.org/10.1162/089120100561610.

Joakim Nivre. 2008. Algorithms for deterministic incremental dependency parsing. *Computational Linguistics* 34(4):513–553. http://wing.comp.nus.edu.sg/ antho/J/J08/J08-4003.pdf.

Kemal Oflazer. 2003. Dependency parsing with an extended finite-state approach. *Computational Linguistics* 29(4):515–544. https://doi.org/10.1162/089120103322753338.

H. S. Sichel. 1974. On a distribution representing sentence-length in written prose. *Journal of the Royal Statistical Society* 137(1):25–34. http://www.jstor.org/stable/2345142.

Warren Teitelman. 1978. *INTERLISP Reference Manual*. Xerox Palo Alto Research Center, Xerox Corporation. (Section 2.2 Using Interlisp – an Overview, 2.4).

Anssi Yli-Jyrä. 2003. Regular approximations through labeled bracketing. In Gerald Penn, editor, *Proceedings of FGVienna: The 8th Conference on Formal Grammar*. CSLI Publications, Stanford University, Stanford, CA, pages 153–166. http://cslipublications.stanford.edu/FG/2003/ylijyra.pdf.

Anssi Yli-Jyrä. 2004. Axiomatization of restricted non-projective dependency trees through finite-state constraints that analyse crossing bracketings. In Geert-Jan M. Kruijff and Denys Duchier, editors, *COLING 2004 Recent Advances in Dependency Grammar*. COLING, Geneva, Switzerland, pages 25–32. https://www.aclweb.org/anthology/W/W04/W04-1504.pdf.

Anssi Yli-Jyrä. 2005. Approximating dependency grammars through intersection of star-free regular languages. *Int. J. Found. Comput. Sci.* 16(3):565–579. https://doi.org/10.1142/S0129054105003169.

Anssi Yli-Jyrä. 2012. On dependency analysis via contractions and weighted FSTs. In Diana Santos, Krister Lindén, and Wanjiku Ng'ang'a, editors, *Shall We Play the Festschrift Game?, Essays on the Occasion of Lauri Carlson's 60th Birthday*. Springer, Berlin Heidelberg, pages 133–158. https://doi.org/10.1007/978-3-642-30773-7_10.

Anssi Yli-Jyrä and Carlos Gómez-Rodríguez. 2017. Generic axiomatization of families of noncrossing graphs in dependency parsing. In *Proceedings of the 55th Annual Meeting of the Association for Computational Linguistics*. Vancouver, Canada, pages 1745–1755. http://aclweb.org/anthology/P17-1160.

Anssi Yli-Jyrä, Jussi Piitulainen, and Atro Voutilainen. 2012. Refining the design of a contracting finite-state dependency parser. In Iñaki Alegria and Mans Hulden, editors, *Proceedings of the 10th International Workshop on Finite State Methods and Natural Language Processing*. Donostia–San Sebastián, Spain, pages 108–115. http://www.aclweb.org/anthology/W12-6218.

Anssi Mikael Yli-Jyrä. 2003. Multiplanarity – a model for dependency structures in treebanks. In Joakim Nivre and Erhard Hinrichs, editors, *TLT 2003. Proceedings of the Second Workshop on Treebanks and Linguistic Theories*. Växjö University Press, pages 189–200.

Multi-tape Computing with Synchronous Relations

Christian Wurm and **Simon Petitjean**
{cwurm,petitjean}@phil.hhu.de

Abstract

We sketch an approach to encode relations of arbitrary arity as simple languages. Our main focus will be faithfulness of the encoding: we prove that with normal finite-state methods, it is impossible to properly encode the full class of rational (i.e. transducer recognizable) relations; however, there is a simple encoding for the synchronous rational relations. We present this encoding and show how standard finite-state methods can be used with this encoding, that is, arbitrary operations on relations can be encoded as operations on the code. Finally we sketch an implementation using an existing library (FOMA).

1 Introduction

There is no need to list the merits and advantages of finite-state methods. However, there are some drawbacks, which are partly due to intrinsic properties of rational (i.e. transducer recognizable) relations in general, partly due to restrictions in current libraries:

1. In general, the rational relations are not closed under intersection and complement. Some libraries offer an approximate version of intersection, but this is not guaranteed to provide accurate results.

2. The question whether given two transducers, the relation recognized by one is a subset of (or equal to) the other is generally undecidable.

3. Standard libraries only support binary relations; we will in fact prove there is no way to faithfully (we will make this precise below) encode rational relations (binary or more than binary) as regular languages by finite-state means.

The goal of this article is to solve all these problems with one step: restrict our attention to synchronous rational relations. This solves problem 1. because this class actually forms a Boolean algebra; it follows that 2. is also solved, as this way, it is easy to decide the inclusion/equivalence problem. We can also solve problem 3., because we can faithfully encode arbitrary n-ary synchronous relations as simple languages. This encoding preserves recognizability (by finite-state automata) and allows to faithfully encode standard operations on relations via (different) standard operations on the code (we will define and explain this in more detail below). As the only drawback, we have to renounce to the additional expressive power of rational relations over synchronous relations; but as it was argued in [9], there might be little actual need for this in linguistic applications.

While from a theoretical point of view, we think there is little to object to our approach, there are large practical obstacles: firstly, synchronous relations are not as comfortable to specify as rational relations: for the latter, the representation of rational expressions is particularly practical and compelling (it is used i.e. by FOMA/XFST). We solve this problem here by defining a subclass of rational expressions which allows us to represent all and only synchronous relations, and we provide a program checking whether an expression is in this class. Secondly, we do not want to build a new program or library from scratch, but rather stick to existing ones. Therefore, we implement an interface which allows to define arbitrary n-ary synchronous relations, which are then encoded as languages and can be passed on to FOMA, a standard automaton library (see [5]). We have to add,

Proceedings of the 13th International Conference on Finite State Methods and Natural Language Processing, pages 41–49,
Umeå, Sweden, 4–6 September 2017. © 2017 Association for Computational Linguistics
https://doi.org/10.18653/v1/W17-4005

however, that the implementation is still work in progress.

Hence we show that we can make use of synchronous relations in finite-state processing without really big obstacles, and this solves the three problems we mentioned above. The paper is structured as follows: next, we lay out the motivations we have sketched here more explicitly. Then we provide the basic definitions of classes of relations and operations on them. Then we sketch our approach and procedure to solve the problems. Finally, we discuss the implementation.

2 Motivation and previous work

We here outline the motivations of this paper more explicitly. It is well-known that rational relations are not closed under intersection (for proof, see [1]), and consequently not under complement. This is problematic for some applications: we might want to intersect two relations, each one implementing a certain set of constraints, where grammatical forms have to satisfy both. Also complementation might be useful, because this way we might specify ill-formed transformations and go from there to well-formed transformations. In fact, libraries as FOMA have a pseudo-intersection operation, but it is not guaranteed to yield a mathematically correct result.[1]

What is more problematic about the lack of intersection and complement is that without them, we cannot decide whether two transducers compute the same relation. This is problematic, because there are many different ways and methodologies to define the same relation. It would be nice to be able to see whether two relations are actually equivalent or one is more permissive than another (e.g. in comparing grammatical frameworks), but this is generally impossible with rational relations: proving equivalence of transducers is equivalent to giving a solution to the Post correspondence problem, which is undecidable (see [4]).

Finally, to our knowledge all existing libraries for transducers and rational relations only support binary relations. This is sufficient for most purposes in grammar engineering: we are interested in input/output relations, for example `word form/morphological analysis`; intermediate steps can and should be discarded. This is no longer true if we are interested in reconstruction of old languages from reported sound changes and shifts: here we often are interested in intermediate forms, and would need a form of "lossless composition" which preserves the intermediate steps. An alternative motivation is for example the desire to include phonology, prosody, semantics etc. into relations. For a nice motivation see [6, 7]. Once we have intersection and arbitrary relations, we also have the possibility to generalize composition by "matching" an arbitrary number of components instead of just one. As this allows to encode intersection, rational relations are obviously not closed under these operations, whereas synchronous rational relations are (for a general definition see below).

The most important previous work on this topic is [7], which also gives an encoding of string tuples of arbitrary size into strings. However, this encoding is somewhat problematic: it either does not preserve recognizability, that is, if an n-ary rational relation is encoded in this way, the code language is not a regular language, or it cannot be computed by a finite automaton (this follows from lemma 4). Moreover, it is not faithful for some operations (see below). This is one main motivation for our approach. Synchronous relations actually have already been used in some applications (see [8]), but in a different library (Vaucanson) and unrelated to the issue of introducing relations of arbitrary arity.

3 Preliminary definitions

There are two equivalent ways to define and represent rational relations, namely firstly as the relations recognized by finite-state transducers, and secondly as the relations denoted by rational expressions. A transducer computes an n-ary relation, if its transitions are labelled by $(\Sigma \cup \{\epsilon\})^n$. For reasons of space, we only formally define rational expressions, and presuppose knowledge of transducers. Fix an arbitrary alphabet Σ and an arbitrary arity n. Then for $a_1, ..., a_n \in \Sigma \cup \{\epsilon\}$, $(a_1, ..., a_n)$ is a rational expression (denoting $\{(a_1, ..., a_n)\}$); moreover if e, f rational expressions, then so are $e \cdot f$ (denoting componentwise concatenation of tuples), $e + f$ (denoting union) and e^* (denoting $1 + e + (e \cdot e) + ...$, where $1 = \{(\epsilon, ..., \epsilon)\}$. A relation is rational if it is denoted by some rational expression; we denote the class by $\mathbf{R}$. The class of synchronous ratio-

---

[1] This intersection is based on identical automaton transitions, but for transducers, these are no longer unique, see [7].

nal relations (**SR**) is more complicated to define: put $\Sigma_\perp := \Sigma \cup \{\perp\}$, for $\perp \notin \Sigma$. The **convolution** of a tuple of strings $(w_1, ..., w_i) \in (\Sigma^*)^i$, written as $\otimes(w_1, ..., w_i)$, is in $((\Sigma_\perp)^*)^i$ and of length $max(\{|w_j| : 1 \le j \le i\})$, is defined as follows: the kth letter-tuple of $\otimes(w_1, ..., w_i)$ is $\langle \sigma_1, ..., \sigma_i \rangle$, where σ_j is the k-th letter of w_j provided that $k \le |w_j|$, and $\perp$ otherwise. The convolution of a relation $R \subseteq (\Sigma^*)^i$ is defined by $\otimes R := \{\otimes(w_1, ..., w_i): (w_1, ..., w_i) \in R\}$. A relation $R \in (\Sigma^*)^i$ is **synchronous regular**, if there is an ϵ-free finite-state automaton with transitions labelled by $(\Sigma_\perp)^i$ recognizing $\otimes R$.

Informally, **SR** are the relations computed by finite-state transducers which allow ϵ-transitions in a component only if no other letter is to follow in this component. There is also a characterization of **SR** in terms of first-order logic (see [2]), which is very convenient as it entails a lot of closure properties, in particular Boolean closure and closure under projection and cylindrification.

To have a more perspicuous notation, we sometimes use the **identity expansion** on languages: for $L \subseteq \Sigma^*$, we have $id(L) \subseteq (\Sigma^*)^2$ with $id(L) = \{(w, w) : w \in L\}$. We thus expand languages to their identity relations. For example FOMA represents every language L as $id(L)$, hence the concept is well-known.

We use **projection** in a slightly different sense than usual, namely in the sense of *projecting away*. We define for $i \le n$, $R \subseteq (\Sigma^*)^n$, $\pi_i(R) = \{(w_1, ..., w_{i-1}, w_{i+1}, ..., w_n) : (w_1, ..., w_n) \in R\}$. We urge the reader to keep in mind that for us, the ith projection is not *choosing* the ith component of tuples, but rather *discarding* it. On binary relations, these two notions of projection are obviously notational variants, but on relations of higher arity, our notion is much more powerful and convenient. The inverse of projections are **cylinders**: for $i \le n + 1$, $R \subseteq (\Sigma^*)^n$, $C_i(R) = \{(w_1, ..., w_{i-1}, v, w_i, ..., w_n) : v \in \Sigma^*, (w_1, ..., w_n) \in R\}$. We can also define C_i as follows: for $R \in (\Sigma^*)^n$, $C_i(R) = \{(w_1, ..., w_{n+1}) : \pi_i(\{(w_1, ..., w_{n+1})\}) \subseteq R\}$; hence cylinders are maximal pre-images of projections. To avoid undefined terms, we introduce the following convention: if $R \subseteq (\Sigma^*)^n$, $i > n$, then $\pi_i(R) = R$, and if $i > n + 1$, then $C_i(R) = R$ (these two conventions are again necessarily parallel, otherwise C_i is no longer an inverse for π_i).

When we encode tuples as strings, relations as languages, the two notions are closely connected to homomorphisms and inverse homomorphisms. We define homomorphisms as follows: $h : (\Sigma^*)^n \to (T^*)^n$ is a homomorphism, if $h(w_1, ..., w_n) = (h(w_1), ..., h(w_n))$, and $h(aw) = h(a)h(w)$. h is a **relabelling**, if $a \in \Sigma$ implies $h(a) \in T$. For a homomorphism $h : \Sigma^* \to T^*$, $L \subseteq T^*$, we write $h^{-1}(L) = \{v \in \Sigma^* : h(v) \in L\}$ for the maximal pre-image. For clarity, we distinguish between a function f and its **graph**, where $graph(f) = \{(x, f(x)) : x \in dom(x)\}$. For every relabelling h, $graph(h)$ is a relation computed by a one-state synchronous transducer. For an arbitrary function $f : M \to N$, $X \subseteq M$, we write $f[X] = \{f(x) : x \in X\}$. Note that if $L \subseteq \Sigma^*$, then $h[L] = \pi_1(id(L) \circ graph(h))$, where $\circ$ denotes relation composition.

A less well-known notion we need to explain is (generalized) **composition** with relations of arbitrary arity. We put, for $R \subseteq (\Sigma^*)^n$, $S \subseteq (T^*)^m$, $o \le m, n$,

$$R \circ_o S = \{(w_1, ..., w_{n-o}, w_{n+1}, ..., w_{(n+m)-o}) : (w_1, ..., w_n) \in R, (w_{n-o}, ..., w_{(n+m)-o}) \in S\}.$$

Hence if $o = 0$, this becomes Cartesian product. Standard composition is $\circ_1$ (usually applied to binary relations), and we will usually write $\circ$ for $\circ_1$. We also define a relative we call **lossless composition**:

$$R \oplus_o S = \{(w_1, ..., w_{n-o}, ..., w_n, ..., w_{(n+m)-o}) : (w_1, ..., w_n) \in R, (w_{n-o}, ..., w_{(n+m)-o}) \in S\}.$$

Hence in this case, the "matching components" are not discarded, but rather kept, this way increasing the arity of the relation; if $m = n = o$, then this becomes intersection. As before, we usually write $\oplus$ instead of $\oplus_1$, which is the standard lossless composition as in [7].

A simple operation is inversion: $R^{-1} = \{(w_n, ..., w_1) : (w_1, ..., w_n) \in R\}$; hence we invert the order of tuples.

Two more standard operations for relations over strings are concatenation and Kleene star: assume $R, S \subseteq (\Sigma^*)^n$. Then $R \cdot S = \{(w_1 v_1, ..., w_n v_n) : (w_1, ..., w_n) \in R, (v_1, ..., v_n) \in S\}$; and $R^* = \{(\epsilon, ..., \epsilon)\} \cup R \cup R \cdot R \cup ....$

The following lemma summarizes the most important closure properties:

Lemma 1 (*SR closure properties*)

1. *If $R, S \subseteq (\Sigma^*)^n$, $R, S \in$ **SR**, then $(\Sigma^*)^n - R, S \cup R, S \cap R \in$ **SR**.*

2. If $R \subseteq (\Sigma^*)^n$, $R \in$ **SR**, then $\pi_i(R), C_i(R) \in$ **SR**.

3. If $R \subseteq (\Sigma^*)^m$, $S \subseteq (\Sigma^*)^n$, $o \leq m, n$, then if $R, S \in$ **SR**, then $R \circ_o S, R \oplus_o S \in$ **SR**.

4. If $R \in$ **SR**, h a relabelling, then $h[R] \in$ **SR**. If h a homomorphism, then $h[L] \in$ **R**.

These results are all well-known and easy to verify, given the logical characterization of **SR** (see [2],[9]): operations in 1. correspond to logical connectives; regarding 2., projection corresponds to existential quantification, cylindrification to introducing new (free) variables. Generalized (lossless) composition in 3. can be easily defined with operations in 1. and 2. (see section 4.2), and claim 4. is obvious.

What is problematic for **SR** is the lack of closure under concatenation and Kleene star: if $R, S \subseteq (\Sigma^*)^n$, $R, S \in$ **SR**, then $R \cdot S$ and R^* need not be in **SR**.

4 Encodings: faithfulness and completeness

4.1 Coding preliminaries

We say a map $\psi : (T^*)^n \to \Sigma^*$ encodes tuples in strings, if there are maps $\phi_1, ..., \phi_n$ such that for all $i : 1 \leq i \leq n$,

(1) $\quad \phi_i(\psi(w_1, ..., w_n)) = w_i$

We write $\vec{x}$ to refer to tuples of strings. This means $\psi(\vec{x})$ contains all relevant information of all components, as they can be uniquely reconstructed. Note that this already entails a number of things, like: for $\vec{x} = (w_1, ..., w_n)$, $(\phi_1(\psi(\vec{x})), ..., \phi_n(\psi(\vec{x})) = \vec{x}$; this in turn shows that ψ is injective. We then say a language $L \subseteq \Sigma^*$ encodes a relation $R \subseteq (T^*)^n$, if $L = \psi[R]$. We define the complexity of the encoding via the complexity of the maps ϕ_i, as these are string-to-string and hence more convenient to handle (but in most natural cases, the complexity of ϕ_i determines that of ψ). An encoding is **simple**, if the maps ϕ_i are relabellings; it is **rational**, if the ϕ_i are finite-state computable. In general, we say a function f is rational if $graph(f)$ is a rational relation. Given an encoding $\psi : (T^*)^n \to \Sigma^*$, $code_\psi := \psi[(T^*)^n]$ denotes the set of code words.

The crucial question for encodings is whether we can faithfully transform operations on relations to operations on the code. Let $R_1, ..., R_n$ be relations, τ be an n-ary operation, ψ be an encoding. Then we say that the operation τ_ψ faithfully encodes τ, if

(2) $\quad \psi(\tau(R_1, ..., R_n)) = \tau_\psi(\psi(R_1), ..., \psi(R_n))$

Hence we can simulate operations on relations by operations on codes. ψ being an injective function already entails that it is faithful for union, intersection and composition; complement easily follows, provided $code_\psi$ is a regular language. For us, the most relevant property of encodings is the following: we want that all standard finite-state methods (FSM) can be faithfully encoded as standard finite-state methods, so if τ is a standard FSM, then τ_ψ should be a standard FSM (though possibly a different one).

We now come to our simple encoding. It is based on tuple concatenation, but not componentwise: we defined $\cdot$ by $(a, b) \cdot (c, d) = (ac, bd)$, which results in a tuple of strings. To encode tuples as strings, we form $(a, b)(c, d)$ (without $\cdot$), which is not a tuple of strings, but rather a string of two tuples. We say that a string of tuples $\vec{x}_1...\vec{x}_i$ is a **factorization** of $\vec{y} \in (\Sigma^*)^n$, if 1. $\vec{x}_1, ..., \vec{x}_i \in (\Sigma \cup \epsilon)^n$, and $\vec{x}_1 \cdot ... \cdot \vec{x}_i = \vec{y}$. Factorizations are thus maximal decompositions, but importantly, factorizations are not unique, because there are factorizations such as $(a, \epsilon)(\epsilon, b)$ of (a, b). What is however unique are **synchronous factorizations**: a factorization $\vec{x}_1....\vec{x}_n$ is synchronous, if the following holds: if the jth letter of $\vec{x}_i$ is ϵ, then for all $m : i \leq m \leq n$, the jth letter of $\vec{x}_m$ is ϵ. Hence synchronous factorizations simply embody the synchronicity condition of synchronous relations, and synchronous factorizations correspond to convolutions, except that the latter are relations, the former are words – which is a crucial difference!

Note: all relations over strings have a unique synchronous factorization, regardless of whether they are synchronous, rational, or even computable. Hence we can conceive of

$$synfact : (\Sigma^*)^n \to ((\Sigma \cup \{\epsilon\})^n)^*$$

as a function, which for every tuple gives its synchronous factorization. This is actually a simple encoding in our sense, where ϕ_i is defined by the relabelling $h(a_1, ..., a_n) = a_i$. Keep in mind however that in factorizations, $(a_1, ..., a_n)$ is treated as an arbitrary letter, just as b. The following result is most important for $synfact$:

Lemma 2 *Assume $R \subseteq (\Sigma^*)^n$. Then R is synchronous rational if and only if $synfact[R]$ is a regular language.*

Proof. The proof is actually straightforward: just interpret a synchronous transducer recognizing a relation as recognizing a language, then you recognize the factorization of the relation, and vice versa. So the transducer remains the same, just its interpretation changes. $\qquad\square$

This lemma is also very useful in order to prove that a relation is not synchronous. For example, take the relation $R_1 = (b, \epsilon)^* \cdot (a, a)^*$. In its synchronous factorization, we have three letters, namely (a, a), (b, a) and (a, ϵ), which for simplicity we write c, d, e. Then the synchronous factorization has the form $synfact(R_1) = \{d^m c^n e^o : m+n = n+o\}$. If we intersect this with $d^* e^*$, then we obtain $\{d^m e^m : m \in \mathbb{N}\}$, which is well-known to be not regular, and hence R_1 is not synchronous. We now provide a useful lemma showing how the maps ϕ_i relate to ψ. We define

$$(3) \quad \langle \phi_1, ..., \phi_n \rangle(w) = (\phi_1(w), ..., \phi_n(w))$$

We extend this to sets in the pointwise fashion.

Lemma 3 *Assume L is regular, and let $\phi_1, ..., \phi_n$ be rational functions. Then $\langle \phi_1, ..., \phi_n \rangle[L]$ is a rational relation.*

Proof. By adding an additional component to $graph(\phi_i)$, it is easy to see that $\{(w, \phi_i(w), w) : w \in \Sigma^*\}$ is a rational relation. Call this (ternary) relation R_{ϕ_i}. By closure under (simple) composition, we can construct $\mathrm{id}(L) \circ R_{\phi_1} \circ ... \circ R_{\phi_n}$, which is an $(n + 2)$-ary relation of the form $\{(w, \phi_1(w), ..., \phi_n(w), w) : w \in L\}$. By using projections π_1, π_{n+2} we obtain $\langle \phi_1, ..., \phi_n \rangle[L]$, which is then still rational (by closure under projection). $\qquad\square$

By closure under inversion, this means that if $\psi(R)$ is finite-state decodable, it is also finite-state encodable: there is an $(n+1)$-ary rational relation $graph(\psi) = \{(w_1, ..., w_n, v) : \psi(w_1, ..., w_n) = v\}$. Now we can state that there does not exist a rational encoding for rational relations:

Lemma 4 *There is no rational encoding $\psi : (\Sigma^*)^n \to T^*$ such that for all rational relations R, $\psi[R]$ is regular.*

Proof. Assume there is such an encoding ψ. An encoding is an injection, hence we have $\psi(R) \cap \psi(S) = \psi(R \cap S)$. Since the encodings $\psi(R)$, $\psi(S)$ are regular, so is $\psi(R) \cap \psi(S) = \psi(R \cap S)$. As ψ can be computed by a finite-state transducer, by closure under transduction and projection, $\langle \phi_1, ..., \phi_n \rangle[\psi(R \cap S)] = \psi^{-1}[\psi(R \cap S)]$ is a rational relation. However, for injective ψ, $\psi^{-1}[\psi(R \cap S)] = R \cap S$, which is the intersection of two rational relations and in general $R \cap S$ might be not rational – contradiction. $\qquad\square$

4.2 Faithfulness for standard operations

After fixing the encoding for relations, we here present the encoding of operations τ_ψ for some standard operations τ. Here it is important to keep in mind: whereas for defining relations, the "tuple structure" of $(a_1, ..., a_n)$ is essential, if we consider languages/factorizations, then $(a_1, ..., a_n)$ is just an arbitrary letter no different from b. For reasons of space, in the following table we write ψ for *synfact*; on the left, we present the operation on (synchronous) relations, on the right the corresponding operation on the code.

τ (on relation)	τ_ψ (on language)
1. $\psi(R \cup S)$	$\psi(R) \cup \psi(S)$
2. $\psi(R \cap S)$	$\psi(R) \cap \psi(S)$
3. $\psi(\overline{R})$	$\overline{\psi(R)} \cap code_\psi$
4. $\psi(\pi_i(R))$	$h_i[\psi(R)]$, h_i a relabelling
5. $\psi(C_i(R))$	$h_i^{-1}(\psi(R))$, h_i a relabelling
6. $\psi(R \circ_1 S)$	$\pi_2(C_3(\psi(R)) \cap C_1(\psi(S)))$
7. $\psi(R \oplus_1 S)$	$C_3(\psi(R)) \cap C_1(\psi(S))$
8. $R \circ_i S$	generalize 6.
9. $R \oplus_i S$	generalize 7.
10. $\psi(R^{-1})$	$h[\psi(R)]$, h a relabelling.

These are the set-theoretic operations (in a wide sense). As regards π and C (projection and cylindrification), these are usually not considered standard operations on relations, but this is only because on binary relations, they do not make too much effect. For our codes/factorizations, they become homomorphisms/inverse homomorphisms: as our letters have the form $(a_1, ..., a_n)$, π_i is simply the relabelling $h_i : ((\Sigma \cup \{\epsilon\})^n)^* \to ((\Sigma \cup \{\epsilon\})^{n-1})^*$, defined by $h_i(a_1, ..., a_n) = h(a_1, ..., a_{i-1}, a_{i+1}, ..., a_n)$; cylindrification C_i becomes the corresponding inverse relabelling h_i^{-1}. We usually do not have homomorphisms directly in our libraries, but we can easily define the one-state synchronous transducers computing them, and obtain the results by composition:

$$(4) \qquad h[L] = \pi_1(\mathrm{id}(L) \circ graph(h))$$

$$(5) \qquad h^{-1}[L] = \pi_2(graph(h) \circ \mathrm{id}(L))$$

So in some way or other, we can easily encode these operations, and hence all these operations can be used without any restriction. What is more serious and problematic are concatenation and Kleene star.

4.3 Concatenation and Kleene star

Our encoding is *not* faithful for concatenation and Kleene star. This is because the concatenation of two synchronous factorizations is not necessarily a synchronous factorization, such as $(a, \epsilon)(\epsilon, a)$. This is related to the fact that synchronous relations are not closed under concatenation, and correspondingly not under Kleene star, so there is no remedy to this problem. Lack of closure under these operations is probably the biggest problem with synchronous relations. We will circumvent this problem by introducing a **category system** of expressions. We can conceive of rational expressions as grammars with just one category, where every combination of categories yields that same category as result. We distinguish three categories of rational expressions:

1. el, the equal-length expressions (all components have equal length)

2. ed, the ϵ-difference expressions, where shorter components are ϵ

3. bd, the bounded difference expressions

4. gd, where difference can be unbounded and shorter components need not be ϵ

5. $\perp$, the expressions which are no longer guaranteed to be synchronous

As we have said, these categories concern the syntactic form of expressions, not their denotation, for which it is just a heuristic. Fix an arbitrary arity; then we have the following syntactic rules:

- $(a_1, ..., a_n) \in el$, if $a_1 \neq \epsilon, ..., a_n \neq \epsilon$

- $(a, ..., a_n) \in bd$ and $(a, ..., a_n) \in ed$ if for some $i \in \{1, ..., n\}$, $a_i = \epsilon$

Note that the assignment is polymorphic, where type polymorphism is handled in the standard way (it can also be avoided by adding a type $ed \wedge bd$). The combinatorics are as follows (we use x as variable for arbitrary categories)

- $el \cdot el = el$

- $el \cdot ed = bd \cdot ed = gd$

- $el \cdot bd = bd \cdot el = bd \cdot bd = bd$

- $el \cdot gd = bd \cdot gd = gd$

- $gd \cdot x = ed \cdot x = \perp$

- $el^* = el$

- $ed^* = ed$

- $bd^* = gd^* = \perp$

Moreover, we define an order $el \leq bd, ed \leq gd \leq \perp$, and for $+$ denoting union, for expressions e, e' of type x, x', $e + e'$ has type $x \vee y$, that is, the join with respect to the order. We call the expressions of category el, bd, ed, gd the **synchronous rational expressions** (SR-expressions); this consequently forms a (proper) subset of the rational expressions We could also devise a more fine-grained and permissive system, but we do not present it for reasons of space. The important thing is the following:

Lemma 5 *Every synchronous rational expression denotes a synchronous rational relation.*

This is easy to prove; for the few critical cases, use the synchronization lemma from [3]. So with SR-expressions, we are on the safe side, though many expressions which do denote synchronous relations are excluded. Note that the problem whether an arbitrary rational expression denotes a synchronous relation is undecidable (see [3], proposition 5.5).

4.4 Completeness of the constructions

Here we prove that with extended SR-expressions (for definition see below), we can construct all and only the synchronous relations. Importantly, this is not to say that only extended synchronous rational expressions denote synchronous relations, but for every synchronous rational relation we can construct an extended SR-expression. Take an alphabet Σ with $|\Sigma| \geq 2$. Let $EL \subseteq (\Sigma^*)^2$ be the set of equal-length string pairs $\{(w, v) : |w| = |v|\}$, $pref \subseteq (\Sigma^*)^2$ the set of pairs $\{(w, wv) : w, v \in \Sigma^*\}$, and for $a \in \Sigma$, $R_a \subseteq \Sigma^*$ the set of strings $\{wa : w \in \Sigma^*\}$. It is easy to see that EL can be constructed as synchronous expression with category el, $pref$ with category $el \cdot ed = gd$, $R_a : a \in \Sigma$ with category el (as it is unary). The completeness of our construction follows from the crucial direction of Eilenberg's result in [2]:

Theorem 6 *(Eilenberg, Elgot, Shepherdson) Assume $|\Sigma| > 1$. Then every synchronous rational relation of arbitrary arity over Σ can be constructed from EL, $\underline{pref}$, $R_a : a \in \Sigma$ by the operations C_i, π_i, $\cup, \cap, \overline{[-]}$.*

Actually, this is slightly different from the original formulation, as we leave out the logic part and only consider the semantics; still our formulation easily follows from the main theorem of [2]. The proof of this statement is long and complicated, so we omit a sketch. We define **extended synchronous expressions** as follows:

- If e is a synchronous rational expression, then it is an extended synchronous rational expression.

- If e, f are extended synchronous rational expressions, then so are $\pi_i(e)$, $C_i(e)$, $e \cap f$, $\overline{e}$.

The interpretation of these expressions is straightforward, as constructors are interpreted as themselves. Now the previous lemmas 1,5 and theorem 6 have the following consequence:

Corollary 7 *A relation R is synchronous regular if and only if it is denoted by some extended synchronous regular expression.*

Of course, our approach so far is rather terse, and there is lots of syntactic sugar we can add; in particular, the operations of (generalized) composition and lossless composition can be added, as they are straightforwardly definable by generalized synchronous expressions. For reasons of space, we do not present this here, but make use of this in our implementation.

5 The procedure and implementation

Of course, it would be possible to construct a library for synchronous relations of arbitrary arity from scratch. This is however not necessary, as our results indicate: we can use a library which is able to handle regular languages and binary relations, and all we have to do is mediate the input:

$$\text{user} \Longleftrightarrow \text{interface} \Longleftrightarrow \text{existing FS-library}$$

Hence the user can interact with our interface, writing relations of arbitrary arity with synchronous rational expressions. The interface encodes them as terms which denote languages (or rather their identity expansion), which are then passed on to an existing library, in our case FOMA. Furthermore, every request by the user is again mediated. These requests can be of different nature:

1. assign the relation in question to a variable, and use it to construct a larger relation

2. check equivalence of two expressions (with or without variables), or emptiness of an expression.

3. check whether a word w is denoted by an expression, or give the output for a certain input, or print some set of tuples which are recognized

These three types of requests can be easily handled, and we quickly sketch the procedure. 1. is easily taken care of, as this is just a variable assignment. 2. emptiness is routinely checked in FOMA; in order to check inclusion $R \subseteq S$, we just have to construct $R \cap \overline{S}$ and check its emptiness. As regards 3., we can just use the standard method constructing the relation $\mathrm{id}(\{w\})$ and compose/intersect, and print the output or check emptiness.

The processing chain of the interface starts with the parsing of the user input. The language that we propose for describing relations is comparable to the one used for regular expressions in FOMA, except that the elementary units are tuples instead of atoms. Before being encoded, the abstract syntax tree resulting of the parsing must be checked, as only synchronous rational expressions will be encoded by the interface.

The checking uses a color system, where colors represent the level of threat to the synchronicity of the relation. Each node in the abstract syntax tree of the expression will be colored either in black, green, orange or red. We start by coloring all the leaves of the tree (the tuples), and then all the colors of the internal nodes of the tree (the operations) are determined depending on the color of their daughter nodes (the arguments of the operations). The checking process explores the tree bottom up until the root, so the whole relation, is given a color. After checking, we will consider that a relation is not synchronous only if its color is red. A tuple will be given the green color if it features an empty word. When a node represents the application of a Kleene star, the resulting color will be orange if its daughter node (its argument) is green, so if the Kleene star is applied to a term containing an empty word. The relation until now is still synchronous, but will not be anymore if anything is concatenated on the right. For this reason, a node is given the red color if it represents a concatenation and if its left daughter node is orange.

One problem still needs to be taken care of after the checking: empty words should not appear in a tuple, except if for all the other tuples concatenated to its right also feature the empty word at the same index. For example, $(a, \epsilon)(a, b)$ should be forbidden. However, $(a, b)(a, \epsilon)$ denotes the same relation, and can be obtained by a simple transformation of the first expression. Our implementation realizes this type of transformation, which we call ϵ-shifting. Whenever two tuples are concatenated, for each empty word in the left tuple, if the word at the corresponding index in the right tuple is not empty, then we swap them. We repeat this process until no ϵ can be shifted anymore.

After checking the expression and performing ϵ-shifting, the encoding can be done. The encoding that we target is actually very close to the string that we had before parsing, due to the similarity between our language and the one of FOMA. The essential difference is that in the target string, we need to make sure that tuples will be interpreted by FOMA as atoms.

Let us now go through the steps of the processing chain while looking at a concrete example. We consider the following input:

((a, epsilon, b) (a, c, a)) | (a, c, b)*

The abstract syntax tree produced by the parser is be as follows:

['union',['concat',[('a','epsilon','b')],
                    [('a','c','a')]],
         ['star',[('a','c','b')]]]

The checking of this tree starts by giving colors to the tuples: (a,epsilon,b) is green because of the ϵ, the two others are black. The concatenation does not produce a red color here, as the left daughter node ([('a', 'epsilon', 'b')]) is not orange but green. It would be the case for example if the input was:

((a, epsilon, b)* (a, c, a)) | (a,c,b)*

In this case, the process would have been stopped after unsuccessful checking. The next step is the ϵ-shifting, which explores the tree looking for concatenations. Only one shift is performed, on:

['concat', [('a', 'epsilon', 'b')],
           [('a', 'c', 'a')]]

The tree which we obtain after the ϵ-shifting is as follows:

['union',['concat',[('a','c','b')],
                    [('a','epsilon','a')]],
         ['star',[('a','c','b')]]]

The encoding part basically does the opposite of what the parser did, unfolding the abstract syntax tree into a string:

((%['a'%,'c'%,'b'%] %['a'%,'epsilon'%,'a'%])
|(%['a'%,'c'%,'b'%])*)

where % is the escape character allowing us to let FOMA consider tuples (here represented as lists) as a single atoms. Now that the output string was produced, the user can compute with FOMA an automaton for the relation. Our interface supports all the operations mentioned in this article, except for composition. This is due to the fact that our interface does not implement its own operations, but uses the ones provided by FOMA, following the translations given in section 4.2. Projection and cylindrification, which are necessary to compute composition, are not supported by FOMA, as they depend on our specific way to encode the tuples. Even though there is no trivial solution for their implementation because of this reason, possible workarounds would include the use of homomorphisms or the development of an extension to FOMA which provides ways to access and modify the elements in our tuples.

6 Conclusion

We have presented an approach to allow users to work with (synchronous) rational relations of arbitrary arity, with full Boolean closure properties and a decidable inclusion problem. Our approach is based on the desire to work with existing libraries, and we have done this by encoding arbitrary relations as simple languages. Our two main results are the following: firstly, an approach as ours cannot work with the full class of rational relations, because it is impossible to encode arbitrary rational relations as regular languages by finite-state means. On the other hand, we have sketched that it works very well with synchronous rational relations, for which only concatenation and star are problematic. The second main result is that we have presented a class of expressions which denotes all and only the synchronous rational expressions, which is not trivial, as the problem whether a rational expression denotes a syn-

chronous relation is undecidable. From a practical
point of view, we have provided a type checker for
expressions and implemented the encoding. However, to provide a full user-interface, some work
still needs to be done.

References

[1] Jean Berstel. *Transductions and Context-free Languages*. Teubner, Stuttgart, 1979.

[2] S. Eilenberg, C. C. Elgot, and J. C. Shepherdson. Sets recognized by n-tape automata. *Journal of Algebra*, 13:447–464, 1969.

[3] Christiane Frougny and Jacques Sakarovitch. Synchronized rational relations of finite and infinite words. *Theor. Comput. Sci.*, 108(1):45–82, 1993.

[4] T. V. Griffiths. The unsolvability of the equivalence problem for λ-free nondeterministic generalized machines. *J. ACM*, 15(3):409–413, July 1968.

[5] Mans Hulden. Foma: a finite-state compiler and library. In Alex Lascarides, Claire Gardent, and Joakim Nivre, editors, *EACL 2009, 12th Conference of the European Chapter of the Association for Computational Linguistics, Proceedings of the Conference, Athens, Greece, March 30 - April 3, 2009*, pages 29–32. The Association for Computer Linguistics, 2009.

[6] Mans Hulden. Grammar design with multi-tape automata and composition. In Thomas Hanneforth and Christian Wurm, editors, *Proceedings of the 12th International Conference on Finite-State Methods and Natural Language Processing, FSMNLP 2015, Düsseldorf, Germany, June 22-24, 2015*. The Association for Computer Linguistics, 2015.

[7] Mans Hulden. Rewrite rule grammars with multitape automata. *Journal of Language Modelling*, To appear.

[8] Florian Lesaint. Synchronous relations in Vaucanson. Technical Report 0833, Laboratoire de Recherche et Développement de L'Epita, 2008.

[9] Christian Wurm and Younes Samih. Synchronous regular relations and morphological analysis. In Mark-Jan Nederhof, editor, *Proceedings of the 11th International Conference on Finite State Methods and Natural Language Processing, FSMNLP 2013, St. Andrews, Scotland, UK, July 15-17, 2013*, pages 35–38. The Association for Computer Linguistics, 2013.

Finite-State Morphological Analysis for Marathi

Vinit Ravishankar
Faculty of ICT
University of Malta
Msida MSD 2080, Malta
vinit.ravishankar@gmail.com

Francis M. Tyers
School of Linguistics
Higher School of Economics
Moscow, Russia
francis.tyers@uit.no

Abstract

This paper describes the development of free/open-source morphological descriptions for Marathi, an Indo-Aryan language spoken in the state of Maharashtra in India. We describe the conversion and usage of an existing Latin-based lexicon for our Devanagari-based analyser, taking into account the distinction between full vowels and diacritics, that is not adequately captured by the Latin. Marathi displays elements of both fusional and agglutinative morphology, which gives us different ways to potentially treat the morphology; philosophically, we approach our analyser by treating the morphology system as a three-layer affixing system. We use the *lttoolbox* lexicon formalism for describing the finite-state transducer, and attempt to work within a morphological framework that would allow for some consistency across Indo-Aryan languages, enabling machine translation across language pairs. An evaluation of our finite-state transducer shows that the coverage is adequate, over 80% on two corpora, and the precision is good (over 97%).

1 Introduction

This paper describes the development of free/open-source morphological descriptions of Marathi, an Indo-Aryan language spoken in the state of Maharashtra in India. Morphological descriptions are computational models of a language's morphology, and are used to output morphological analyses from word forms and vice versa.

In section 2, the paper gives an overview of Marathi morphology, and talks about some of the grammatical decisions we made during development of the analyser. Section 3 is a literature review of previous work done in the field. Section 4 describes the methodology we followed whilst working on the analyser, the formalisms we have used, and describes our lexicon. We continue with section 6, describing the evaluation metrics we

have chosen, and how well our analyser performs on them. Section 7 describes potential future work we could do.

2 Marathi

Marathi is an Indo-Aryan language spoken primarily in the west Indian state of Maharashtra, and has approximately 62 million speakers, as of 2003 (Pandharipande, 2003). Despite being an Indo-European language, Marathi has borrowed several features - such as clusivity, and certain retroflex consonants (such as the retroflex lateral flap), either absent or relatively uncommon in other Indo-Aryan languages.

Whilst Marathi retains some fusional morphological aspects of its proto-language, Sanskrit, it displays morphological agglutination within many contexts. Our analysis broadly follows the perspective of Masica (1993). They consider the split morphological to be a form of morphological "layering"; with a primary layer, comprising mainly of inherited fusional elements (the "oblique" case), a secondary agglutinative layer, and a tertiary postpositional layer. These layers are, to a certain extent, universal amongst Indo-Aryan languages: they differ largely in the conditions under which they occur, and language-specific variations that may occur. A brief, specific definition of the layers in Marathi would, therefore, look like:

1. The "oblique" case; complex morphophonemic changes in the lemma. eg. मुलगा *mulaga* "boy" → मुला *mula*

2. Agglutinative suffixes, similar to traditional cases that mark noun functions, like the nominative or the genitive.

3. Postpositions; morphologically and semantically complex elements. These can attach to an (optional) oblique genitive suffix in layer 2.

Certain particles, such as an emphasis particle -च -*c*, or particles like -ही -*hī* and -सुद्धा -*suddhā* "as well as", are quite common, and can attach as a suffix to most words, with the exception of conjunctions. Verbs, along with the optional negation particle, decline for

Proceedings of the 13th International Conference on Finite State Methods and Natural Language Processing, pages 50–55,
Umeå, Sweden, 4–6 September 2017. © 2017 Association for Computational Linguistics
https://doi.org/10.18653/v1/W17-4006

tense, aspect and mood, and have adjectival and adverbial derivations. (1) is an example with two of the three case layers and two suffix particles.

(1) (to) ghar-ā-māge-hī
     (he) house-OBL-behind.POST-too.PTCL
     ge-l-ā-c
     go-PFV-3MSG-FOC
     "He definitely went behind the house too"

3 Prior work

There have been a number of efforts to develop morphological analysers for Marathi over the years. While morphological analysis for Marathi is fairly well studied, one downside of previous work is that the software and lexicon is not freely available. Dixit et al. (2005) present a spellchecker for the language based on a lexicon of 13,000 root words and morphological rules. They did an evaluation of spell-checking accuracy showing that out of 10,648 words classified as correctly spelt, only 0.45% were actually false positives. The morphological analyser of Bapat et al. (2010) is based on a word–paradigm approach modelled with a finite-state transducer and contains a lexicon of 24,035. They evaluate 21,096 unique word forms from a corpus and find that 97.18% receive all and only the correct morphological analyses; it is worth noting, however, is that their dictionary was created to specifically fit their evaluation corpus. Another analyser based on finite-state technology is described by Dabre et al. (2012), based on a gold standard of 1,341 words, achieved an accuracy of 72.18%. The size of the lexicon was not specified. Gawade et al. (2013) also use a finite-state transducer to model Marathi morphology, although their paper does not evaluate its effectiveness.

Resources like BabelNet[1], generated by statistically machine translating WordNet ontologies, do not appear to be very useful - whilst BabelNet does contain some Marathi nouns, common verbs are all absent.

4 Development

We initially worked on the open word classes, many of which could be successfully scraped from the resources of the Language Technologies Research Centre (LTRC), at the International Institute of Information Technology, Hyderabad.[2] As the lexicon was in WX notation,[3] a transliteration script was used along, along with standard UNIX command line utilities, to extract and convert noun paradigms. Adjective paradigms were fairly trivial to convert; a significant number of adjectives do not inflect at all, and most others are very

---

[1] http://babelnet.org/
[2] Available from the LTRC website at `http://ltrc.iiit.ac.in/showfile.php?filename=onlineServices/morph/index.htm`
[3] WX is an ASCII-based transliteration scheme for Indian languages; the name derives from the use of 'w' and 'x' for dental stops.

regular. Words were then *scraped* (extracted) from the lexicon and assigned to their respective paradigms.

Verbal declensions were stored with a different method; separate files existed, not for separate paradigms, but for separate word forms. Each file had a set of words, declined to match the particular form described by the file. The lexicon, however, was similar to the nominal lexicon, in that verbs were assigned a particular verb paradigm. Rather than merge these multiple files into a single paradigm, we created our own verbal paradigms, with Dhongade and Wali (2009) and Masica (1993) as references. The verb list, however, primarily consists of entries from the LTRC lexicon.

4.1 Formalisms

For the finite-state transducer we employ the *lttoolbox* formalism, an XML-based format used in the *Apertium* project (Forcada et al., 2011). This formalism is widely used for encoding language data, with Apertium having over 40 language pairs for machine translation. Although we could have used an FST toolkit like HFST (Lindén et al., 2011) or Foma (Hulden, 2009), with separate layers for processing morphonology and morphotactics, the lack of significant morphophonological processes relevant to Marathi orthography made *lttoolbox* a perfectly adequate choice.

4.2 Lexicon

The main source of lexical material for our analyser is from an existing morphological analyser published by the Language Technology Research Centre (LTRC) at IIIT Hyderabad. Unlike other work on Marathi, the lexicon is available under the free/open-source GPL licence. The source lexicon (see example in Figure 3) is composed of a dictionary table containing six columns. All text in Marathi is written in a Latin-based transliteration scheme.

The paradigms in the LTRC lexicon are essentially lists of different forms of a word; words are assigned paradigms based on their conformance to the inflection of the paradigm word. One of the biggest problems with this is the inefficient noun paradigm system; each paradigm lists forms that include bound postpositional morphemes (including adjectival postpositions); this is quite unnecessary, as postpositions (layer 3) are largely regular, and attach to the oblique case (layer 1) with an optional clitic (layer 2). This results in 968 forms per paradigm, where four would suffice - the singular and plural nominative and oblique. There were other minor problems, such as the inclusion of plural forms for uncountable nouns or abstract nouns.

4.3 Paradigms

The Apertium paradigm system essentially functions using finite-state transducers, defined in XML. Paradigms are expressed as an input side (within '<l></l>' tags), and a corresponding output side (within '<r></r>' tags); the transducer is made to re-

```
^ठेचा/ठेचा<n><m><sg><nom>$
^मिरची/मिरची<n><f><sg><nom>$
^,/,<cm>$
^चिंच/चिंच<n><f><sg><nom>$
^व/व<cnjcoo>$
^मीठापासून/मीठ<n><nt><sg><obl>+पासून<post><adv>$
^तयार केला/तयार करणे<vblex><perf><p3><m><sg>$
^जातो/जाणे<vblex><impf><p3><m><sg>$
^./.<sent>$
```

Figure 1: Example output from the analyser for the sentence ठेचा मिरची, चिंच व मीठापासून तयार केला जातो *ṭhēcā miracī, ciṃnca va mīṭhāpāsūna tayāra kelā jāto* "Pickles are prepared using chilis, tamarind and salt." Note that the example has been manually disambiguated for brevity. The tag `cnjcoo` is coordinating conjunction, and `cm` is comma.

turn the lemma of a word and the corresponding tags. The Marathi dictionary had a few caveats regarding transliteration of the lexicon to Unicode; a paradigm with the invariant part of the word ending before a vowel would require additional entries in Unicode, depending on whether the final letter of the invariant part was a vowel sound or not. For instance, consider the pair *A/I* and *t/I*: the Unicode equivalents for this pair would be आ/ई and त/ी, with the vowel displayed as a diacritic in the second case. Both characters — the full vowel and the diacritic — are distinct Unicode code points. Whilst we can *infer*, from the WX transliteration equivalent, that the vowel ought to be a diacritic and not a full vowel, the distinction is explicit in the Unicode.

For several morphological contexts in which Marathi displays some form of agglutinativity, we have used the "join" operator, which essentially redirects the FST to another paradigm after it consumes the input for the first. This has resulted in a lot of 'minor' paradigms in the dictionary.

There are significant phonological differences between spoken and literary Marathi; these often reflect in informal written Marathi, which tends to modify spellings to match the spoken variant. Most paradigms include, therefore, multiple forms mapping onto the same analysis; there are, however, restrictions placed on the non-standard forms to prevent them from being generated during morphological generation. The most common example of this is neuter agreement - whilst literary Marathi uses the vowel /e/ ँ *e* to mark the third-person neuter, informal Marathi uses a schwa, represented by a nasalisation diacritic ँ.

5 Grammar

During the development of this analyser, we made several linguistic decisions, some of which we shall attempt to describe and justify.

5.1 Light verbs

Marathi, like many other Indo-Iranian and Turkic languages, has frequent light verbs. These are, essentially,

noun + verb constructs that represent a verbal predicate. These constructs have been fairly widely studied, particularly within the context of Persian (Karimi-Doostan, 2005). Whilst N + V combinations are, by far, the most common type of construct, there are several constructs where the first element cannot exist as an independent term (but are glossed as adverbs). (2) is an example of a sentence with a light verb construction, using the relatively uncommon verb मारणे *mārṇe* "to hit".

(2) mī (zamīn-ī-lā) zhāḍū mār-t-o
    I (floor-OBL-DAT) broom.N hit.V-IPFV-1MSG
    I sweep (the floor)

In our analyser, we attempt to create separate entries for every semantically valid light verb pair - i.e., an entry for each noun + verb combination, with a whitespace token separating the two. Whilst this approach does make things easier from the perspective of machine translation, it has two disadvantages - it is very laborious work, and it is not completely compatible with other linguistic resources, like the Universal Dependencies treebank project (Nivre, 2015), which requires that both the noun and the verb have separate analyses. We intend to eventually add support for both forms of analysis; Figure 2 shows the difference between the two analyses.

5.2 Verbal morphology

An issue we faced during development of the analyser was finding suitable names for all verb forms. Marathi's relative verbal complexity, and the lack of consistency amongst our reference grammars along with the absence of descriptions of several verb forms, made this a fairly difficult task. We describe some of the forms:

- **Supine:** `<sup>`; name derived from the Latin supine, these forms indicate purpose for the action denoted by the verb; i.e. "in order to" carry out the action.

- **Transgressives:** `<trans>`; similar to Slavic transgressives, the forms indicate simultaneous (imperfective) and consecutive (perfective) actions.

- **Inceptives:** `<incp>`; inceptives typically form compounds with the verb लागणे *lāgṇe* "to attach", and indicate the starting of the action denoted by the verb.

- **Predictive:** `<pred>`; these forms indicate an *intent* to carry out the action denoted by the verb.

```
^तयार करणे/तयार करणे<vblex><inf>$
^तयार/तयार<adv> करणे/करणे<vblex><inf>$
```

Figure 2: Example analyses for the light verb construct तयार करणे *tayār karṇe* "to prepare". The first analysis is what we use; the second is an intended addition.

Corpus	Tokens	Cov. (%)	Mean ambig.
Wikipedia	4.0M	80.2	1.7
Bible	751K	80.7	1.9
Average	–	80.45	1.8

Table 1: Corpora used for naïve coverage tests

	Precision	Recall
Known tokens	0.97	0.97
All tokens	0.97	0.71

Table 2: Precision and recall over all tokens and only known tokens. Out of 699 tokens which were checked, the stems of 347 were not in the lexicon.

The same forms are also used for the desiderative, to imply a desire to do something - we, however, chose to use `<pred>`, similar to Dhongade and Wali (2009).

It is worth noting that gerunds[4], like nouns, can take affixes functionally similar to the second and third layer in nominal affixing. The gerund itself is assumed to be the oblique, and therefore does not undergo any further modification before it takes case or postpositional suffixes. (3) is an example of a gerund with a postposition.

(3) tu-jhyā   basṇ-yā-nantar   mī ge-l-o
    you-GEN sit-GER-after.POST I go-PFV-1MSG
    I went after you sat *(after your sitting)*

6 Evaluation

We have evaluated the morphological analyser in two ways. The first was by calculating the naïve coverage and mean ambiguity on freely available corpora. Naïve coverage refers to the percentage of surface forms in a given corpora that receive at least one morphological analysis. Forms counted by this measure may have other analyses which are not delivered by the transducer. The mean ambiguity measure was calculated as the average number of analyses returned per token in the corpus.

Our analyser was also used by Ravishankar (2017) to evaluate coverage on generated back-transliterated corpora; their coverage was comparable to our evaluation, at 72.65% for their best system.

6.1 Corpora

We used two freely-available corpora for the evaluation. The first is the Marathi Wikipedia,[5] and the second is the Bible in Marathi.[6]

6.2 Precision and recall

Precision and recall are measures of the average accuracy of analyses provided by a morphological transducer. Precision represents the number of the analyses given for a form that are correct. Recall is the percentage of analyses that are deemed correct for a form (by comparing against a gold standard) that are provided by the transducer. To calculate precision and recall, it was necessary to create a hand-verified list of surface forms and their analyses. We extracted 1,000 unique surface forms at random from a Wikipedia corpus, and checked that they were valid words in the languages and correctly spelled. Where a word was incorrectly spelled or deemed not to be a form used in the language, it was discarded.

This list of surface forms was then analysed with the most recent version of the analyser, and each analysis was checked. Where an analysis was erroneous, it was removed; where an analysis was missing, it was added.[7] This process gave us a 'gold standard' morphologically analysed word list of 699 forms. The list is publicly available for each language in Apertium's SVN repository.

We then took the same list of surface forms and ran them through the morphological analyser once more. Precision was calculated as the number of analyses which were found in both the output from the morphological analyser and the gold standard, divided by the total number of analyses output by the morphological analyser.

Recall was calculated as the total number of analyses found in both the output from the morphological analyser and the gold standard, divided by the number of analyses found in the morphological analyser plus the number of analyses found in the gold standard but not in the morphological analyser.[8]

The results for precision and recall are presented in table 2.

6.3 Qualitative

After performing the manual evaluation, we found that a majority (59.6%) of the missing analyses were nouns or proper names. For the former class, the missing analyses were often English loanwords; amongst these, we rejected ones that would not conventionally occur in

---

[4]Dhongade and Wali (2009) do not treat these forms as gerunds; we disagree.

[5]The dump file used was `mrwiki-20150901-articles.xml.bz2` from `http://dumps.wikimedia.org`.

[6]Downloaded from `https://www.wordproject.org/bibles/mar/`. Corpus statistics and coverage are presented in table 1.

[7]By this we mean that analyses which the morphological analyser produced which were erroneous were removed from the gold standard in order to be able to determine how frequently the analyser produces erroneous analyses.

[8]For example, for the surface form *wound* in English, if the gold standard has {`wound<n><sg>`, `wind<vblex><pp>`, `wind<vblex><past>`, `wound<vblex><inf>`, `wound<vblex><pres>`} and the output of the morphological analyser is {`wound<n><sg>`, `wound<vblex><inf>`, `wound<vblex><pres>`} then the recall will be $\frac{3}{3+2} = \frac{3}{5} = 0.6$.

Marathi. Compound nouns were also quite common; many of these were loanwords from Sanskrit, a language with significant compounding, or from Perso-Arabic. For proper nouns, the missing analyses are easily explainable by the fact that many foreign names are not part of the lexicon, and by the fact that we have not yet split proper names into multiple paradigms: we assume similar inflectional paradigms for all of them.

Amongst the incorrect analyses, a few were due to our duplication of the -त -*t* suffix; we treated it as both the locative case, and as a postpositional suffix. Both have exactly the same semantic meaning, and treating it as a case suffix is largely due to convention and dialectal differences. Most other errors were ambiguities between verbs and nouns. There were also several errors with distinctions between verbal adverbs and postpositional adverbs; this distinction was removed in subsequent revisions of the analyser.

7 Future work

Most of our future work will involve expanding the size of the lexicon to improve coverage. Two specific domains, however, would make for interesting future expansions:

7.1 Apertium

By modifying the morphology standards to fit the entire Indo-Aryan language family, creating rule-based machine translation systems across Indian languages would be an interesting future project. The syntactic differences between Indo-Aryan languages are relatively more minor than the morphological differences, which make them very suitable to Apertium's chunking-based transfer system.

7.2 Universal Dependencies

The Universal Dependencies project (Nivre, 2015) is a collection of dependency parsed treebanks in several languages. The ConLL-U format used by UD contains, along with dependency labelling, fields with morphological analyses of each word. Using Apertium's morphological analyser, along with a script to automatically convert Apertium-style tags to UD-style tags, would simplify the process of creating a Marathi treebank.

8 Conclusions

We have presented, to our knowledge, the first free/open-source morphological descriptions for Marathi. The analyser has reasonable coverage over two available test corpora, and the precision is high (over 0.97).

Acknowledgements

We would like to thank the anonymous reviewers for their insight and helpful comments. We would also like to thank Memduh Gökırmak for inspiring discussion. The first author of this paper is funded by a stipend from the Erasmus Mundus Language and Communication Technology programme.

Column					
1	2	3	4	5	6
boWatapaNe		AVY	avy		
wAra		basa	v		
pusakata		hAwa	adj		
tAMgava		basava	v		
anuBavI		AVY	avy		
meNekarI		BikArI	nm		

Figure 3: A random sample of entries in WX notation from the LTRC Marathi lexicon. The first column is the stem, the third column is the inflection paradigm name, and the fourth column is the part of speech (avy *uninflected*, v *verb*, adj *adjective*, nm *masculine noun*). The second, fifth and sixth columns are not relevant to our work.

References

Bapat, M., Gune, H., and Bhattacharyya, P. (2010). A paradigm-based finite state morphological analyzer for Marathi. In *Proceedings of the 1st Workshop on South and Southeast Asian Natural Language Processing (WSSANLP)*, pages 26–34.

Dabre, R., Amberkar, A., and Bhattacharyya, P. (2012). Morphological analyzer for affix stacking languages: A case study of Marathi. In *COLING 2012, 24th International Conference on Computational Linguistics, Proceedings of the Conference: Posters, 8-15 December 2012, Mumbai, India*, pages 225–234.

Dhongade, R. and Wali, K. (2009). *Marathi*. London Oriental and African language library. John Benjamins Publishing Company.

Dixit, V., Dethe, S., and Joshi, R. K. (2005). Design and implementation of a morphology-based spellchecker for Marathi, an Indian language. *Archives of Control Sciences*, 15:301–308.

Forcada, M. L., Ginestí-Rosell, M., Nordfalk, J., O'Regan, J., Ortiz-Rojas, S., Pérez-Ortiz, J. A., Sánchez-Martínez, F., Ramírez-Sánchez, G., and Tyers, F. M. (2011). Apertium: a free/open-source platform for rule-based machine translation. *Machine Translation*, 25(2):127–144.

Gawade, P., Madhavi, D., Gaikwad, J., Jadhav, S., and Ambekar, R. (2013). Morphological analyzer for Marathi using NLP. *International Journal of Engineering Research and Applications*, 3(2).

Hulden, M. (2009). Foma: a finite-state compiler and library. In *Proceedings of the 12th Conference of the European Chapter of the Association for Computational Linguistics: Demonstrations Session*, pages 29–32. Association for Computational Linguistics.

Karimi-Doostan, G. (2005). Light verbs and structural case. *Lingua*, 115(12):1737–1756.

Lindén, K., Axelson, E., Hardwick, S., Pirinen, T. A., and Silfverberg, M. (2011). Hfst—framework for compiling and applying morphologies. In *International Workshop on Systems and Frameworks for Computational Morphology*, pages 67–85. Springer.

Masica, C. (1993). *The Indo-Aryan Languages*. Cambridge Language Surveys. Cambridge University Press.

Nivre, J. (2015). Towards a universal grammar for natural language processing. *Computational Linguistics and Intelligent Text Processing*, 9014:3–16.

Pandharipande, R. (2003). Marathi. In Cardona, G. and Jain, D., editors, *The Indo-Aryan Languages*, pages 698–728. Routledge, Abingdon.

Ravishankar, V. (2017). Finite-State Back-Transliteration for Marathi. *The Prague Bulletin of Mathematical Linguistics*, 108(1).

Word Transduction for Addressing the OOV Problem in Machine Translation for Similar Resource-Scarce Languages

Shashikant Sharma and Anil Kumar Singh
IIT (BHU), Varanasi, India
{shashikant.sharma.cse12, aksingh.cse}@iitbhu.ac.in

Abstract

Similar languages have a large number of cognate words which can be exploited to deal with Out-Of-Vocabulary (OOV) words problem. This problem is especially severe for resource-scarce languages. We propose a method for 'word transduction' for addressing this problem. We take advantage of the fact that, although it is difficult to prepare sentence aligned parallel corpus for such languages, it is much easier to prepare 'parallel' list of word pairs which are cognates and have similar pronunciations. We can try to learn pronunciations (or orthographic representations) of OOV words from such a parallel list. This could be done by using phrase-based machine translation (PBMT). We show that, for small amount of data, a model based on weighted rewrite rules for phoneme chunks outperforms a PBMT-based approach. An additional point that we make is that word transduction can also be used to borrow words from another similar language and adapt them to the phonology of the target language.

1 Introduction

Current research in the field of Automatic Speech Recognition (ASR) and Machine Translation (MT) tends to focus on the language pairs that have a large amount of data available. This is because the quality of these systems is dependent on the amount and quality of the training data used. As a result, many such systems between (relatively) resource-rich languages, such as English, Hindi, and Urdu are available. However in a country like India, there are 122 major languages and over 1599 other languages spoken by different communities[1]. Most of these languages are resource-scarce and therefore very little or no work has been done on these languages. Language is one of the major factors responsible for digital divide between urban and rural areas due to prevalence of information technology in urban areas (Dubey and Devanand, 2013). Therefore, removing this language barrier is crucial to the growth of the society as well as for bridging the digital divide.

Hindi has several 'dialects' (often called sub-languages) spread over the entire Hindi speaking region commonly known as the Hindi-Belt. Bhojpuri is one of the seven Hindi sub-languages (other six include Awadhi, Braj, Haryanvi, Bundeli, Bagheli and Kannauji) (Mishra and Bali, 2011). Although the designation of Bhojpuri as a language or simply as a dialect of Hindi is a topic of debate[2], it is closely related to Hindi and borrows many words from Hindi, either directly or with some phonological (and thus, orthographic) changes. Besides, both use the Devanagari script for all official purposes, which (like major Indian languages, Indo-Aryan and Dravidian) has evolved from the ancient Brahmi script (Sproat, 2002; Sproat, 2003). In spite of having more than 33 million speakers[3], Bhojpuri is a resource-scarce language due to lack of resources such as machine readable dictionaries, WordNet and any standard parallel corpus, which makes the development of machine translation (MT) systems very challenging. For the same reason, Statistical Machine Translation is not feasible as it requires a

---

[1] http://www.censusindia.gov.in/Census_Data_2001/Census_Data_Online/Language/gen_note.html
[2] http://ncictt.com/index.php/articles/42-bhojpuri-a-dialect-of-hindi
[3] http://www.censusindia.gov.in/Census_Data_2001/Census_Data_Online/Language/Statement1.aspx

Proceedings of the 13th International Conference on Finite State Methods and Natural Language Processing, pages 56–63,
Umeå, Sweden, 4–6 September 2017. © 2017 Association for Computational Linguistics
https://doi.org/10.18653/v1/W17-4007

large parallel corpus. Alternatively, direct MT is more suitable for closely related languages (Hajič et al., 2000).

Therefore, preparation of sufficient amount of data for NLP tools like MT systems seems very difficult in the near future. Any such system, due to lack of resources, faces low-coverage issues due to the presence of unknown (Out-Of-Vocabulary or OOV) words.

To address this issue, we propose a 'word transduction' approach, which can show noticeable improvement in inter-dialectal translation by transducing OOV words. We define the term word transduction as the conversion of words from one source language to another closely related target language such that pronunciation and meaning are similar. This can have two aspects. One is cognate generation, while the other is adapting borrowed words from the source language to the target language such that it matches the phonology of the target language. In other words, word transduction can be seen as transliteration (Denoual and Lepage, 2006; Finch and Sumita, 2009) *in the same script* to incorporate phonological changes between a pair of closely related languages.

Since the problem of machine transliteration can also be viewed as the process of machine translation at the character level, we have used the popular phrase-based SMT (Statistical Machine Translation) system Moses between Hindi-Bhojpuri word pairs as the baseline system. SMT requires a bilingual parallel training data, a language model (LM), a translation model (TM) and a decoder. This method uses mapping of small text chunks (called 'phrases') without the utilization of any explicit linguistic information (such as morphological, syntactic, or semantic). That is, it considers only the surface form of words to create a phrase table. Such additional information can be incorporated in the form of 'factors', along with the words or characters (in case of transliteration) to improve the accuracy of standard SMT.

Surface form, along with these factors, creates factored representation of each word (Koehn et al., 2007; Koehn and Hoang, 2007). For factored SMT, we augmented each letter of Devanagari with their phonetic features (described in the next section) to create its factored representation. This factored Statistical Machine Translation at character level performed better than our baseline SMT system.

The representation of speech using a sequence of phonetic symbols is defined as transcription. Hindi has a phonetic writing system, i.e., there is very little distinction between its transcription and pronunciation. Therefore, it is reasonable to assume that words in Hindi and Bhojpuri are spelled or transcribed in the same way as they are pronounced (Choudhury, 2003). This property makes the mapping of Devanagari letters to International Phonetic Alphabet (IPA) symbols very easy. IPA is organized in such a way that each symbol on a chart can be visualized as a hierarchical structure of features (Peter Ladefoged, 1988). It is possible to decomposes letters in the IPA representation into the building block of sounds (features). We have used the IPA representation of both source (Hindi) and target (Bhojpuri) language. For instance, क is a single Devnagari alphabet but is equivalent to क् + अ, i.e., क has the inherent vowel अ which is easily reflected in its IPA representation(/kə/).

The major contributions of this paper are:

- We propose a phoneme chunk based method for word transduction which transduces words of Hindi to its closely related language Bhojpuri. Using the method described in this paper, we try to predict Bhojpuri pronunciation from its corresponding Hindi word. This method is adapted from extensively reported earlier work on similar problems.

- We also show that proposed phoneme chunk based method for word transduction performs better than the standard Statistical Machine Translation as well as factored Statistical Machine Translation (Koehn and Hoang, 2007) when applied on the same dataset using the Moses decoder (Koehn et al., 2007).

2   Related Work

In a parallel corpus of a language and its dialect (or closely related language), words can be categorized into two categories based on their pronunciation or orthographic form:

- Word pairs having entirely different pronunciations (and hence orthographic forms) in the two varieties. For example, रउआ (rauaa) in Bhojpuri means आप (aap, you-honorific) in Hindi. This type of word pairs share almost no or very little phonetic and orthographic similarity. Since our model utilizes phonetic transition between two closely related languages, this type of word-pairs are not suitable for our model.

- Words having similar pronunciations (and hence their orthographic forms). A phonemic study of Hindi and Bundeli (Acharya, 2015), mainly focusing on the prosodic features and the syllabic patterns of these two languages concluded that the borrowing of words from Hindi to Bundeli generally follows certain rules. For instance if a word in Hindi starts with य [ya], it is replaced by ज [ja] in its Bundeli equivalent as यजमान [yajamaan] becomes जजमान [jajamaan], यमुना [yamunaa] becomes जमुना [jamunaa] etc. This category of word-pairs is our main motivation behind the work described in this paper. Our goal was to build a system which takes a word as input in one language and returns its equivalent in some other language which is closely related to source language by using the phoneme to phoneme conversion. The next section will describe the steps of the proposed method.

Koo (2011) proposed a model using weighted finite state transducers (WFST) to implement phoneme rewrite rules for English to Korean. This finite state model was applied to predict how English words and named entities are pronounced in Korean by a native speaker of Korean. Initially the model keeps one or more rewrite rules for every phoneme in English, then each rewrite rule specializing in a given English phoneme is weighted according to the probability with which the rule applies. Each rewrite rule is defined as:

$$\phi \rightarrow \varphi / \lambda\_\rho$$

i.e., rewrite ϕ as φ when preceded by λ and followed by ρ. ϕ is an English phoneme, φ is a phoneme of Korean. In other words, these rules, consisting of three basic operations, can be implemented as the union of three WFSTs, i.e., deletion, substitution and substitution plus insertion. Koskenniemi (2013) modelled correspondences between two historically related languages (Finnish and Estonian, derived from Proto Balto-Finnic or PBF) using finite state transducers (FST). Using general linguistic knowledge, Finnish and Estonian forms were aligned letter by letter with each other and these aligned words, known as Aligned Finnish-Estonian (AFE),

were used as a substitute for the proto-language. AFE, having more symbols than the normal set of phonemes (as in PBF), was applied to produce Finnish, Estonian and PBF directly and unambiguously.

Singh (2006) formulated a phonetic model to represent relations between the sounds of Indian languages and the letters or 'akshars' (orthographic syllables). It included phonetic features (Clements, 1985) mapped to each letter as well as a computational model to calculate the orthographic and phonetic distance between given pair of akshars, letters, words or strings. The phonetic features described were mainly the ones considered in modern phonetics, as well as some orthographic features specific to Indian language scripts. The distance measure was based on the fact that phonetic features differentiate two sounds (or akshars representing them) in a cascaded or hierarchical way. The features that we have used for factored SMT are selected from the higher levels only, since the Moses decoder only allows four factors at most. These features, along with their possible values, are listed in Table 1.

Features	Possible Values
Type	Unused, Vowel modifier, Nukta, Halant, Vowel, Consonant, Number, Punctuation
Height (vowels)	Front, Mid, Back
Sthaan (place)	Dvayoshthya, Dantoshthya, Dantya, Varstya, Talavya, Murdhanya, Komal-Talavya, Jivhaa-Muliya, Svaryantra-mukhi
Prayatna (manner)	Sparsha, Nasikya, Parshvika, Prakampi, Sangharshi, Ardh-Svar

Table 1: Phonetic features and their possible values

3 Proposed Model

Previous studies have shown that we can use weighted finite state transducers (WFST) to generate rewrite rules for translation between closely related languages (Koskenniemi, 2013) as well as to generate phonological rules (Koo, 2011; Gildea

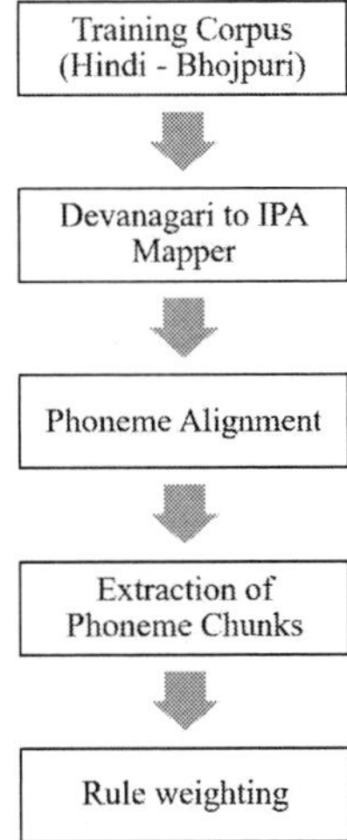

Figure 1: Structure of the Training Model

and Jurafsky, 1995) for word pronunciation. However, when the implementation of a method similar to Koo (2011) was applied on Hindi-Bhojpuri parallel list, it yielded poor results. This was due to the fact that model proposed by Koo considered only single phonemes of the source language (English) while formulating the rewrite rules. Our proposed method, instead of considering single phonemes, considers rewrite rules of all possible chunks and weights them according to the frequency of occurrence in the dataset. Furthermore, general rewrite rules were defined using regular expressions to post-process the ranked output from the trained model.

3.1 Training the Model

The structure of the training model is shown in the figure 1. Each of these steps is described in detail below:

1. **Devanagari to International Phonetic Alphabet Converter.** Using the assumption that Devanagari alphabets have the same pronunciation and transcription, we can map each Devanagari letter to their equivalent IPA using a freely available mapping[4]. This mapping is mostly one-to-one as each Devanagari letter has a unique mapping to IPA and vice-versa. Phoneme length of a word is the count of these IPA units. For example [bʱ] for भ is a single phoneme. Note that phoneme length

[4] https://en.wikipedia.org/wiki/Help:
IPA_for_Hindi_and_Urdu

and character length are two different terms which will be used later during alignment of phonemes. Consider the following examples:

Example 1: लगे (/ləgeː/) has $character\ length\ =\ 5$ and $phoneme\ length = 4$

Example 2: डगमगाना (/ɖəgəməgaːnaː/) has $character\ length\ =\ 12$ and $phoneme\ length = 10$

2. **Alignment of the source and the target words for rule extraction.** This is the key step for our model. In this step, we align phonemes of word pairs in such a way that it has minimum phonetic distance (Singh, 2006). In our case, Hindi is the source language and Bhojpuri is the target language. These word pairs may have different phoneme lengths and, therefore, three types of rewrite rules are possible: *Substitution, Deletion and Insertion*. Put differently, a rewrite rule in this case defines how a Hindi phoneme should be edited via deletion, substitution, or insertion depending on which phoneme appears on both sides. For example, डगमगाना (/ɖəgəməgaːnaː/) → डगमगाइल (/ɖəgəməgaːilə/) have one phoneme insertion and two phoneme substitutions.

We redefine an IPA representation of Hindi-Bhojpuri word pairs by inserting a placeholder ε until phoneme length of both source and target becomes equal and have minimum possible phonetic distance. For example, /ɖəgəməgaːna → /ɖəgəməgaːilə/ after alignment becomes /ɖəgəməgaːɛnaː/ → /ɖəgəməgaːilə/. Since Hindi-Bhojpuri word pairs now have equal phoneme length, only one type of rewrite rule, i.e., substitution is required.

3. **Extraction of Phoneme Chunks.** From aligned training data, we extract phoneme chunks (phoneme n-grams). We enumerate all possible phoneme substrings of the Hindi word for a given Hindi-Bhojpuri aligned pair. Since phoneme length is the same, a phoneme chunk of Hindi will directly map to a phoneme chunk of Bhojpuri of the same length (see figure 2). For example, after alignment with its Bhojpuri translation, परेम (/pəreːmə/), प्रेम (/preːmə/) will have the IPA representation /pɛreːmə/ and the constituent

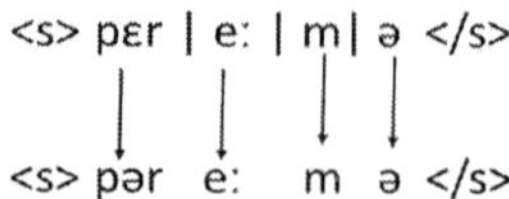

Figure 2: Mapping Hindi phoneme chunks to Bhojpuri phoneme chunks.

phoneme chunks can be generated as shown in Table 2.

Hindi	Bhojpuri
<s> p | ɛre:mə <s>	<s> p | əre:mə <s>
<s> pɛ | re:mə <s>	<s> pə | re:mə <s>
<s> pɛr | e:mə <s>	<s> pər | e:mə <s>
<s> pɛre: | mə <s>	<s> pɛre: | mə <s>
<s> pɛre:m | ə <s>	<s> pəre:m | ə <s>
<s> p | ɛ | re:mə <s>	<s> p | ɛ | re:mə <s>
<s> ..... <s>	<s> ..... <s>

Table 2: Some entries of the aligned phoneme chunks for word प्रेम (each phoneme chunk is separated by "|", and <s> is a word boundary marker)

4. **Rule weighting.** Each phoneme chunk can be transduced to phonemes of a Bhojpuri word of the same length as shown in figure 3. Therefore, each rewrite rules derived will be of the form:

$$\alpha \to \beta$$

where α is a phoneme chunk of Hindi and β is a Bhojpuri phoneme chunk of the same length. Rule derivation process after alignment consists of finding the probability of chunk translation and weighting each translation based on its weight W, defined as:

$$W(\alpha \to \beta) = (p(\alpha \to \beta))^2 * plen(\alpha)$$

where $plen(\alpha)$ is the phoneme length of α and $p(\alpha \to \beta)$ is the probability of translation α to β, calculated as:

$$p(\alpha \to \beta) = \frac{C(\alpha \to \beta)}{C(\alpha)}$$

$C(\alpha \to \beta)$ means the frequency of α translated to β in aligned phoneme chunks of training data and $C(\alpha)$ means a count of all the occurrences of α in aligned phoneme chunks of training data. Probability p was considered only if $p \geq 0.50$.

3.2 Estimating Bhojpuri Pronunciation

Estimating Bhojpuri pronunciation consists of two steps. Using weighted Hindi phoneme chunks, we first assign a rank to each possible translation, then we treat the phonemic representation of the highest ranked word from this output as an input to the general rewrite rule system. Put differently, as explained earlier, first all possible phoneme chunks are enumerated for the Hindi word whose Bhojpuri pronunciation is to be estimated, then for each row in aligned phoneme chunks (see Table 2), each of the phoneme chunks are tranduced to Bhojpuri and their weights are aggregated to calculate the rank of the transduced output. Highest ranked output is then passed as an input to the general rewrite rule system, which relies on the linguistic knowledge about the Bhojpuri language. This system consists of mapping of Hindi phonemes to Bhojpuri using regular expressions, and some of its rewrite rules are given below:

- $k\underline{s} \to c^h$
- $\eta \to n$
- $\varsigma \to s$
- $v \to b$
- $:rj \to j$
- $<s>j \to <s>j$ ($<s>$ is a boundary marker for the start of a word)
- $\underline{s} \to s$
- $v\theta \to v\partial\theta$ (both v, θ are phonemic equivalent of a consonant)

4 Experiments

Experiments were performed from two points of view: the accuracy test and the phonetic distance comparison.

4.1 Dataset

The proposed model was trained and tested using a dataset consisting of 4220 Hindi-Bhojpuri word pronunciation pairs chosen from a lexicon compiled by language experts. The 4220 pairs were randomly split into a training set and a test set in a three-to-one ratio. The model was developed on 3165 pronunciation pairs and predicted the Bhojpuri pronunciation of Hindi words in the remaining 1055 pairs. Dataset consisted of word pairs of Type 2 words (described in Section 2). A sample of the corpus is shown in Table 3.

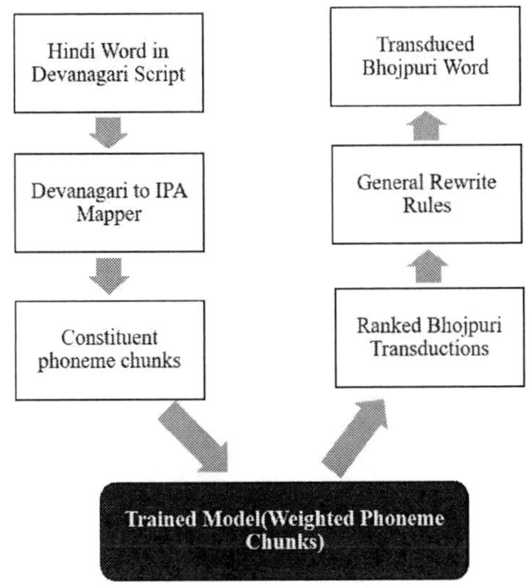

Figure 3: Estimating Bhojpuri Pronunciation from a Hindi word.

Hindi	Bhojpuri
किस्मत (kismata)	किसमत (kisamata)
ढिंढोरा (dhindhoraa)	ढिनढोरा (dhinadhoraa)
सताता (sataataa)	सतावल (sataavala)
विकसित (vikasita)	बिकसित (bikasita)
स्कूल (skUla)	इसकूल (iskUla)
कौआ (kau-aa)	कउआ (ka-u-aa)

Table 3: Sample word pairs from dataset (Roman transliteration in parenthesis)

4.2 Statistical Machine Translation

For this work, a bilingual Hindi-Bhojpuri Machine Translation Model has been used as the baseline by using the Moses decoder. Moses requires a parallel corpus (e.g. Hindi and Bhojpuri) that is used for training the system. For this task, each letter from the parallel corpus (parallel word list) of Hindi-Bhojpuri language pair was treated as if it was a word of a sentence and each word was treated as a single sentence. In other words, machine translation was performed at the character level. The publicly available tool GIZA++ was used to align the letters (Och and Ney, 2003). IRSTLM (Federico et al., 2008) was used to create the language model, which computes the probability of target language sentences (words in our case). Language model was prepared using the 19532 words, compiled from a Bhojpuri newspa-

per[5] and (a very limited) Hindi-Bhojpuri parallel corpora.

4.3 Factored Statistical Machine Translation

Moses (Koehn et al., 2007) provides framework for statistical translation models that easily integrates additional linguistic informations as factors. For the purpose of word transduction, each Devanagari letter was provided with its phonetic features to create its factored representation. As phonetic features differentiate between two sounds in a cascaded or hierarchical way, features were selected based on the level of hierarchy. Since the hard limit of factors in Moses is 3, we considered two different sets of phonetic features - the first set (we name it FSMT1) had features named Type, Height and Prayatna (manner), and the second one (we name is FSMT2) had Type, Height and Sthaan (place). This factored parallel corpus was then used to train the translation model using the SMT tools (Moses decoder, GIZA++ and IRSTLM).

Method	Word Accuracy (WA)
SMT	53.022%
FSMT1	54.746%
FSMT2	54.989%
Proposed Method	64.411%

Table 4: Word Accuracy Test

4.4 Evaluation Measures

Accuracy was measured by the percentage of the number of correctly transduced words divided by total number of generated transductions. We term it as word accuracy (WA). We define one more measure, called normalised phonetic distance (NPD) that measures the phonetic distance between a correct word and a generated word.

$$WA = \frac{Number\ of\ correct\ translation}{Total\ number\ of transduced\ words}$$

$$NPD(T, B) = \frac{PD(T, B) - PD_{min}}{PD_{max} - PD_{min}}$$

where $PD(T, B)$ is phonetic distance between transduced output T, and correct transduction B, computed using phonetic model as described by Singh (2006), PD_{min}, PD_{max} are minimum and maximum phonetic distance between transduced

[5]http://tatkakhabar.com/

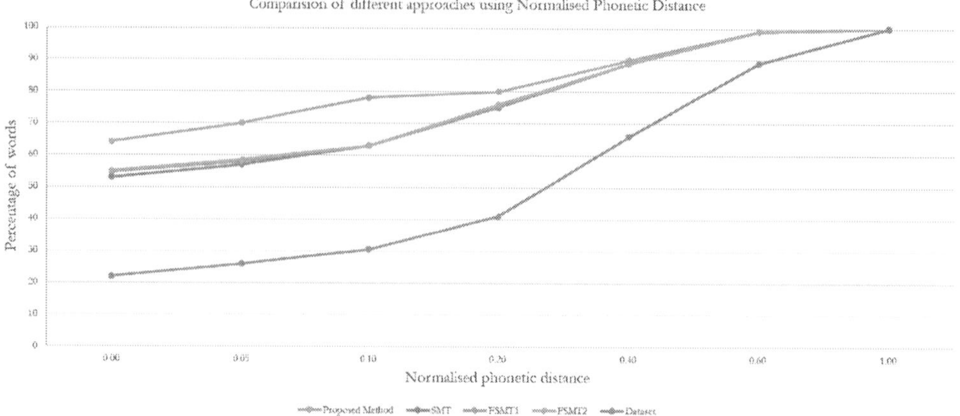

Figure 4: NPD comparison between proposed method and SMT on the same training and test dataset.

output and correct translation in the test corpus, respectively.

4.5 Accuracy Test

We compare our results to word accuracy of SMT and factored SMT in Table 4, which concludes that factored SMT with phonetic features as the factors performs better than standard SMT. However our phoneme chunk based method performs better than the other methods. This could be because we do not have enough data for SMT, which is the common scenario for resource-scarce languages.

4.6 BLEU Score

The BLEU score (Papineni et al., 2002) (which is one of the most popular measures for machine translation) for all the methods is summarised in Table 5. Here also our method significantly outperforms other methods for our language-pair.

Method	BLEU Score
SMT	75.05
FSMT1	75.92
FSMT2	76.18
Proposed Method	79.82

Table 5: BLEU score comparison

4.7 Normalised Phonetic Distance Test

We compare two methods also on the basis of Normalised Phonetic Distance (NPD). This test has physical significance in terms of pronunciation difference between generated output and the correct translation. The higher the value of accuracy

for a given NPD, the closer the pronunciation of the transduced word and the correct transduction. We evaluated normalised phonetic distance (NPD) for five different word pairs:

1. Hindi-Bhojpuri word pairs of the test corpus (shown by the curve $Dataset$ in Figure 4)

2. Generated output by the SMT technique and its correct Bhojpuri output (shown by the curve SMT in Figure 4)

3. Generated output by the FSMT1 technique and its correct Bhojpuri output (shown by the curve $FSMT1$ in Figure 4)

4. Generated output by the FSMT2 technique and its correct Bhojpuri output (shown by the curve $FSMT2$ in Figure 4)

5. Generated output by the proposed technique and its correct Bhojpuri output (shown by the curve $Proposed\ Method$ in Figure 4)

From the comparison we can conclude that proposed method has better performance than SMT in reducing the pronunciation difference for the data size that we have.

5 Conclusion

We proposed an approach ('word transduction') for addressing the OOV problem for resource-scarce similar languages, of which one is more resource-scarce. Word transduction is aimed at guessing the pronunciation or the orthographic form of the target word, given the source word.

We learn to do this from a parallel list of cognate words. The approach can also be useful for adapting borrowed words to the phonology of the target language. We showed that a weighted rewrite rule-based method on phoneme chunks significantly outperforms a method based on factored phrase-based machine translation for this purpose for such language pairs. For future work, we plan to improve the implementation to make it faster and also to prepare more data so that the transducer can become practically useful, e.g. in an MT system. We are also trying Deep Learning methods for comparison. We plan to extend the dataset we have used and to release it for further work.

References

Ankita Acharya, 2015. *Contrastive Study of Bundeli and Hindi Pronunciation*. regICON-2015: Regional Symposium on Natural Language Processing, Varanasi.

Monojit Choudhury. 2003. Rule-based grapheme to phoneme mapping for hindi speech synthesis. In *90th Indian Science Congress of the International Speech Communication Association (ISCA), Bangalore, India*.

George N Clements. 1985. The geometry of phonological features. *Phonology*, 2(01):225–252.

Etienne Denoual and Yves Lepage. 2006. The character as an appropriate unit of processing for non-segmenting languages. In *NLP Annual Meeting*, pages 731–734.

Preeti Devanand Dubey and Devanand. 2013. Machine translation system for hindi-dogri language pair. In *Machine Intelligence and Research Advancement (ICMIRA), 2013 International Conference on*, pages 422–425. IEEE.

Marcello Federico, Nicola Bertoldi, and Mauro Cettolo. 2008. Irstlm: an open source toolkit for handling large scale language models. In *Interspeech*, pages 1618–1621.

Andrew Finch and Eiichiro Sumita. 2009. Transliteration by bidirectional statistical machine translation. In *Proceedings of the 2009 Named Entities Workshop: Shared Task on Transliteration*, pages 52–56. Association for Computational Linguistics.

Daniel Gildea and Daniel Jurafsky. 1995. Automatic induction of finite state transducers for simple phonological rules. In *Proceedings of the 33rd annual meeting on Association for Computational Linguistics*, pages 9–15. Association for Computational Linguistics.

Jan Hajič, Jan Hric, and Vladislav Kuboň. 2000. Machine translation of very close languages. In *Proceedings of the sixth conference on Applied natural language processing*, pages 7–12. Association for Computational Linguistics.

Philipp Koehn and Hieu Hoang. 2007. Factored translation models. In *EMNLP-CoNLL*, pages 868–876.

Philipp Koehn, Hieu Hoang, Alexandra Birch, Chris Callison-Burch, Marcello Federico, Nicola Bertoldi, Brooke Cowan, Wade Shen, Christine Moran, Richard Zens, et al. 2007. Moses: Open source toolkit for statistical machine translation. In *Proceedings of the 45th annual meeting of the ACL on interactive poster and demonstration sessions*, pages 177–180. Association for Computational Linguistics.

Hahn Koo. 2011. A weighted finite-state transducer implementation of phoneme rewrite rules for english to korean pronunciation conversion. *Procedia-Social and Behavioral Sciences*, 27:202–208.

Kimmo Koskenniemi. 2013. Finite-state relations between two historically closely related languages. In *Proceedings of the workshop on computational historical linguistics at NODALIDA 2013; May 22-24; 2013; Oslo; Norway. NEALT Proceedings Series 18*, number 087, pages 53–53. Linköping University Electronic Press.

Diwakar Mishra and Kalika Bali. 2011. A comparative phonological study of the dialects of hindi. In *Proceedings of International Congress of Phonetic Sciences XVII*, pages 1390–1393.

Franz Josef Och and Hermann Ney. 2003. A systematic comparison of various statistical alignment models. *Computational Linguistics*, 29(1):19–51.

Kishore Papineni, Salim Roukos, Todd Ward, and Wei-Jing Zhu. 2002. Bleu: a method for automatic evaluation of machine translation. In *Proceedings of the 40th annual meeting on association for computational linguistics*, pages 311–318. Association for Computational Linguistics.

Morris Halle Peter Ladefoged. 1988. Some major features of the international phonetic alphabet. *Language*, 64(3):577–582.

Anil Kumar Singh. 2006. A computational phonetic model for indian language scripts. In *Constraints on Spelling Changes: Fifth International Workshop on Writing Systems*. Nijmegen, The Netherlands.

Richard Sproat. 2002. Brahmi scripts. In *Constraints on Spelling Changes: Fifth International Workshop on Writing Systems, Nijmegen, The Netherlands*.

Richard Sproat. 2003. A formal computational analysis of indic scripts. In *International symposium on indic scripts: past and future, Tokyo*.

A FST Description of Noun and Verb Morphology of Azarbaijani Turkish

Razieh Ehsani   **Berke Özenç**   **Ercan Solak**

Işık University, Istanbul, Turkey

`name.surname@isikun.edu.tr`

Abstract

We give a FST description of nominal
and finite verb morphology of Azarbaijani Turkish. We use a hybrid approach
where nominal inflection is expressed as
a slot-based paradigm and major parts of
verb inflection are expressed as optional
paths on the FST. We collapse adjective
and noun categories in a single nominal
category as they behave similarly as far as
their paradigms are concerned. Thus, we
defer a more precise identification of POS
to further down the NLP pipeline.

1 Introduction

Azarbaijani Turkish (AT) is a Turkic language
spoken by more than 30 million people mainly
in Iran and Azarbaijan. AT is an agglutinative
language with rich and regular inflectional and
derivational morphologies. As in all Turkic languages, vowel harmony and consonant changes at
the morpheme boundaries are conditioned by the
phonological context. Word order is relatively free
and the syntactic relations are indicated by case
markings and in spoken form also by stress.

The alphabet has 23 consonants, adding ç, ş, ğ
to the consonants of the Latin alphabet and removing w from it. It has 9 vowels, adding ı, ü, ö and ə
to the Latin alphabet. The Table 1 gives the front-
ness, roundness and height of vowels.

	Front		Back	
	Flat	Round	Flat	Round
Close	i	ü	ı	u
Mid	e	ö		o
Open	ə		a	

Table 1: Vowels and their properties

There are a few morphological analyzers for
Turkish, (Oflazer, 1994), (Çöltekin, 2010), (Şahin
et al., 2013) and Turkic languages like Turkmen
(Tantug et al., 2006), Kazakh (Kessikbayeva and
Cicekli, 2016), Uighur (Orhun et al., 2009). Although, AT is close to the Turkish spoken in
Turkey, there are enough non-trivial differences
both in morphotactics and phonology to prevent
the direct use of analyzers implemented for Turkish. To the best of our knowledge, this work is
the first FST implementation of AT noun and finite verb inflections.

In our implementation, we used Helsinki FST,
(Lindén et al., 2011). We provide the details of the
full FST as supplementary materials. The present
description involves nominal and verb inflections
in isolation. We are extending this initial effort to
the rest of the AT morphology and we will make
the full implementation publicly available as a web
service.

2 Approach

For each morpheme, we represent its abstract
form either as a key-value pair for slot-based
paradigms or just as a key for other paradigms. For
example, <Case:Abl> denotes an abstract morpheme for ablative case. The first level of morphology yields the archmorphemes prior to the
phonological transformations in the second level.
Thus, in FST description, a transition expressed
as <Case:Abl>:-NAn yields the archmorpheme
-NAn where the archiphoneme 'N' stands for a
choice of 'n' or 'd' and 'A' stands for 'a' or ə.

3 Nominal inflection

The nominal inflection in AT has a fixed order of
suffixes as

Nominal stem + Number + Possessor + Family +
Case.

Nominal stem may be either a simple nominal

Proceedings of the 13th International Conference on Finite State Methods and Natural Language Processing, pages 64–68,
Umeå, Sweden, 4–6 September 2017. © 2017 Association for Computational Linguistics
https://doi.org/10.18653/v1/W17-4008

root or a complex form that has already undergone a series of derivations.

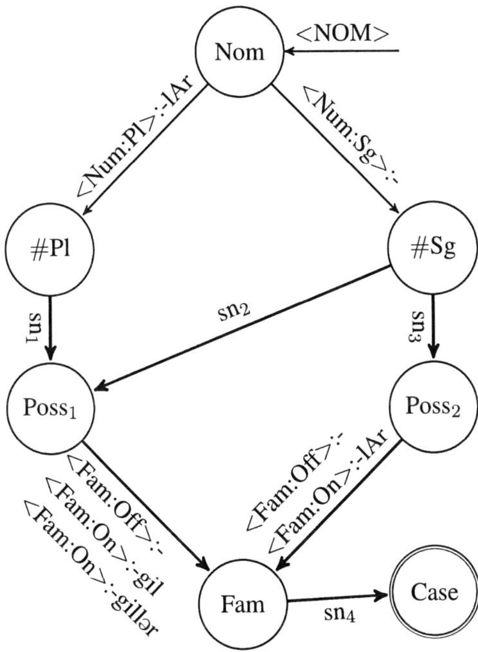

Figure 1: Slot-based nominal inflection in AT

The Number slot can have Singular or Plural values where Singular has zero surface form. There are 7 values for the Possessor key including the value None for no possessor. The Case slot may have values Nominal, Accusative, Dative, Locative, Ablative, Genitive and Instrumental.

The Family slot is binary valued as On/Off. We could have represented it as an optional morpheme without a slot. However, as we wanted to represent all of nominal inflection as slot based, we used the binary value trick to represent its presence.

When On, the surface realizations of the Family slot are one of -gil, -gilǝr or -lAr. Note that the third form -lAr is the same as the surface realization of Plural morpheme. The collision of surface realizations is the reason for the occurrence of such seemingly irregular forms as

(1) xala-m-lar   xala-lar-ım
     aunt-P1SG-PLU   aunt-PLU-P1SG

The apparent reordering of the possessor and plural suffixes in (1) seems to contradict the strictly ordered paradigm of nominal inflection. However, the semantics of the two forms (1) indicate the presence of two distinct morphemes with the same surface forms. Indeed, while "xala-lar-ım" means "my aunts", "xala-m-lar" means "the family of my aunt" or "my aunt and her group." The analysis with the family slot becomes more apparent when we use the other family suffix -gil

(2) xala-m-gil   *xala-gil-im
     aunt-P1SG-FAM   aunt-FAM-P1SG

where the family suffix is forced to come after possessor.

The FST for the nominal paradigm is given in Figure 1.

The possessor morphemes sn_1, sn_2 and sn_3 in Figure 1 are listed in Table 2. Note that some morphemes such as <poss:2p> have multiple equivalent surface forms.

Abstract morpheme	First level output		
	sn_1	sn_2	sn_3
<Poss:None>	-	-	-
<Poss:1s>	-Im	-(I)m	-(I)m
<Poss:2s>	-In	-(I)n	-(I)n
<Poss:3s>	-I(n)	-(s)I(n)	
<Poss:1p>	-ImIz	-(I)mIz	
<Poss:2p>	-InIz	-(I)nIz	
	-Iz	-(I)z	
<poss:3p>	-I(n)	-lArI(n)	

Table 2: Possessor person paradigms for Figure 1. Empty cells are undefined. Apart from epenthesis, the only difference between sn_1 and sn_2 is <Poss:3p>.

Since our nominal inflection paradigm is slot-based, the only accepting state is the Case. The case symbols for sn_4 are of the form <Case:v>:a where (v,a) pair is one of (Nom,-), (Dat,-(y)A), (Loc, -dA), (Acc, -(n)I), (Abl, -NAn), (Gen, -(n)In) and (Ins, -(y)InAn).

4 Verbal paradigm

The inflection of finite verbs also has a fixed order with few exceptions mainly due to the copulas. In its general form, the verb paradigm is

Verb stem + Voice + Ability + Polarity + Probability + Tense-aspect-mood + Person.

The whole paradigm is quite complex. In order handle the complexity, we divided the paradigm into smaller sub-paradigms with clear interfaces among them.

4.1 Voice

There are 5 voices, Active, Reflexive (Rflx), Reciprocal (Rcpr), Causative (Caus) and Passive (Pasv). Apart from Active voice, each has a variety of surface realizations which are specified lexically or phonologically. A verb stem might have multiple voices under co-occurrence and ordering restrictions. The ordering of the voices are

(Reciprocal or Reflexive) + Causatives + Passive.

Theoretically, the Causative voice marker can be repeated freely to denote an arbitrarily long chain of causation. However, in practice, only up to three Causative markers are used.

The FST for the voice paradigm is shown in Figure 2. The Causative and Passive morpheme symbols sv_1, sv_2 and sv_3 in Figure 2 are listed in Table 3.

Symbol	Morpheme
sv_1	<Caus>:-Irt
	<Caus>:-Art
	<Caus>:-(I)t
sv_2	<Caus>:-dIr
sv_3	<Pasv>:-(I)l
	<Pasv>:-(I)n

Table 3: Voice suffixes

state. In order not to clutter the diagram, we showed only two of these, the ones from $Caus^3$ and $Caus_A^2$. There are two distinct paths for multiple causatives, the path $Caus_A^1$-$Caus_A^2$-$Caus^3$ and $Caus_B^1$-$Caus_B^2$-$Caus^3$. These are conditioned by the phonotactics of the different causative suffixes. However, it is difficult to come up with rules governing the choice of a particular causative suffix. Less common suffixes are best represented as being conditioned by the verb stem lexicon. Note that there are 4 allomorphs (rows sv_1 and sv_2 in Table 3) for causative and 2 (row sv_3) for passive when they are attached immediately after the verb stem. In our implementation, we created 15 distinct initial states to handle their possible combinations (including no Passive and no Causative) and we marked the correct transition within the verb lexicon. We refrained from using flag diacritics at the expense of increasing the number of states.

4.2 Ability, Polarity, Probability

The interaction among Possibility, Polarity and Probability is given in the FST in Figure 3. The multiple paths for polarities are needed for the different Person paradigms of negative Aortive tense. The symbol <Abil> denotes the Ability abstract morpheme. Similarly, <Prbl> denotes Probability morpheme. <Pol:Pos> and <Pol:Neg> denote positive and negative polarity morphemes, respectively. <Pol:Pos> has zero surface realization.

In AT, there are two morphemes with the same canonical surface forms to express Possibility and Probability. These respectively correspond to 'be able to' and 'might' in English. Similarity of surface forms precludes their adjacency. So, it is impossible to morphologically compose 'he might be able to come' in AT. Instead, we end up with an ambiguous construction that expresses either possibility or probability. However, when the negative polarity suffix -mA is in between, we can say

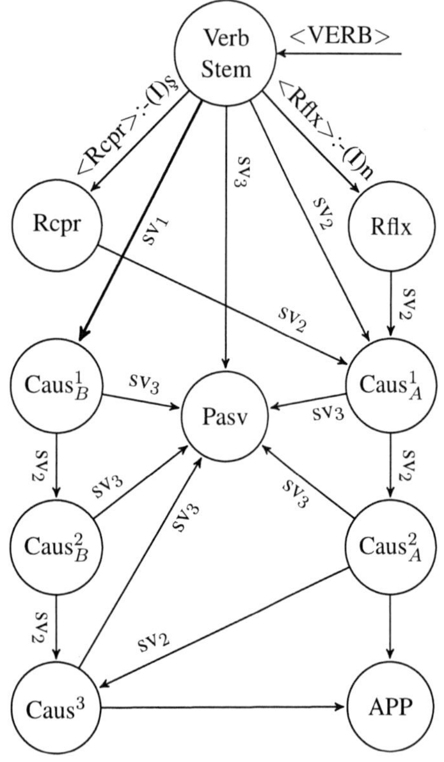

Figure 2: Voice paradigm

The APP state in Figure 2 represents the state connecting the Voice FST to the part of the verb inflection paradigm which deals with Ability, Polarity and Probability given in Figure 3. We treat the transitions within the voice paradigm as optional so all the states have an edge to APP

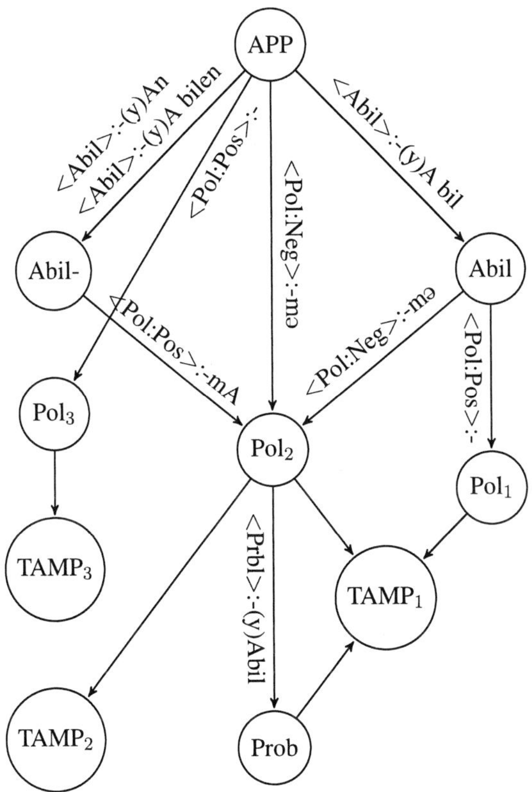

Figure 3: Ability-Polarity-Probability

(3)   gəl-ə bilən-mə-yebil-ər
       come-ABIL NEG-PROB-AOR-3SG
       he might not be able to come.

The standard orthography of AT has a split of the word before the surface form 'bilən' of Ability morpheme. Furthermore, there are two more allomorphs -(y)An and -(y)A bilən of Ability morpheme when it is followed by negative polarity.

The states labeled as $TAMP_1$, $TAMP_2$ and $TAMP_3$ in Figure 3 are the states connecting the FST describing Ability, Polarity and Probability to the FST describing Tense, Aspect, Modality and Person (TAMP) which is partially given in Figure 4. Note that the transitions to TAMP states do not output anything.

4.3 Tense, Aspect, Modality and Person

The last paradigm of finite verb inflection has the basic order

Tense + Copula + Person + Condition + Question.

Only Tense and Person are obligatory and the rest are optional. The order of Copula and Person changes in some cases.

In AT, often a single morpheme expresses a combination of tense, aspect and modality (TAM). There are 11 tenses. In terms of their interactions with their surrounding context, we grouped them into 9 distinct groups. There are 4 copula morphemes corresponding to Aortive, Narrative, Past and Conditional.

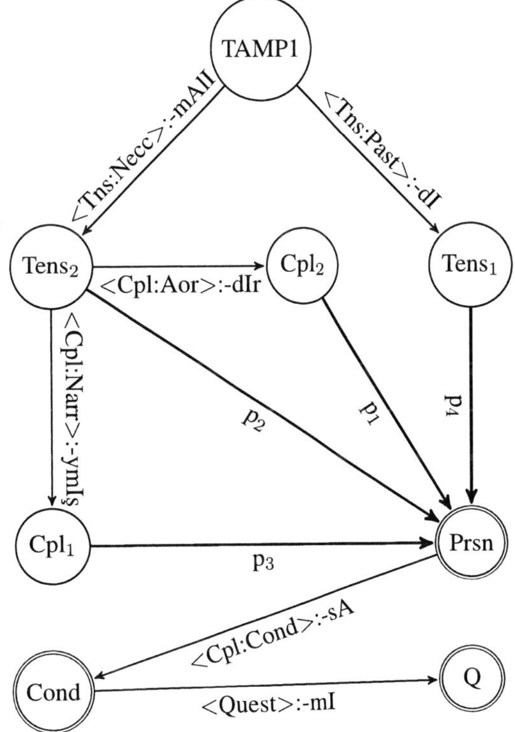

Figure 4:   Tense-aspect-mood and person paradigm for Past and Necessity tenses.

The FST for the full TAM-Person paradigm is too complicated to present in the body of the present paper. We provide in Figure 4 only a part of it to show different paths for copula and person paradigms. We provide the full paradigm in the supplementary materials.

Person	p_1	p_2	p_3	p_4
<Prsn:1s>		-yAm	-Am	-m
<Prsn:2s>		-sAn	-sAn	-n
<Prsn:3s>	-		-	-
<Prsn:1p>		-yIQ	ıQ	-q
<Prsn:2p>		-sInIz	-sInIz	-nIz
<Prsn:3p>	-lAr		-lAr	-lAr

Table 4: Person morphemes in Figure 4.

In Figure 4, <Tns:Past> and <Tns:Necc> represent abstract morphemes for Past and Necessity tenses, respectively. <Cpl:Narr> and <Cpl:Aor> represent the copula morphemes for Narrative and Aortive.

The possible person suffixes p_1-p_4 are listed in Table 4. Note that <Prsn:3s> has zero surface realization. The empty cells in columns p_1 and p_2 show that following Necessity tense, the Aortive Copula is possible only for singular or plural third person.

5   Phonology

In AT, the rules governing phonemic changes depend mostly on the phonological context, enabling an almost complete decoupling of morphotactics and phonology in the implementation. In our implementation, however, we embedded some of the phonological rules in the morphotactics FST whenever the phonological context is known.

There are two major categories of phonological rules in AT. The first one deals with the insertion of epenthetic letters (y), (n) and (s). In our implementation, we start with epenthetic letters inserted by default and drop them when needed. The second major category deals with the mapping of archiphonemes, A, I, N, Q and K to their surface forms. We list the rules below in the order they are applied.

1. Epenthetic (y) and (s) drop when they follow a consonant.
2. Epenthetic (n) drops when it is the last letter in a word.
3. The negative suffix -mA drops its A before a vowel or (y).
4. The archiphoneme N maps to n when it follows n or m, it maps to d otherwise.
5. The archiphoneme A is mapped to surface phonemes to satisfy back-front harmony. It maps to a when it is the first vowel after a back vowel and it maps to ə when following a front vowel.
6. The archiphoneme I maps to u, ü, ı or i for round-flat and back-front harmony.
7. The archiphoneme Q maps to the archiphoneme K when it follows a front vowel. K is further mapped according to the next rule.
8. The archiphoneme Q maps to ğ and the archiphoneme K maps to y before a vowel.

6   Conclusion

We provided HFST descriptions of the nominal and finite verb inflections of Azarbaijani Turkish. Our specification of nominal inflection resolves the apparent reordering of possessive and plural morphemes using a new family/group morpheme.

Currently, we are working on working out the rest of the morphology complete with derivation, nominal predicates and a root lexicon. After unifying the isolated parts in a single analyzer, we plan to make its implementation publicly available and also present the analyzer as a web service.

References

[Çöltekin2010] Çağrı Çöltekin. 2010. A freely available morphological analyzer for Turkish. In *Proceedings of the 7th International Conference on Language Resources and Evaluation (LREC 2010)*, pages 820–827.

[Kessikbayeva and Cicekli2016] Gulshat Kessikbayeva and Ilyas Cicekli. 2016. A Rule Based Morphological Analyzer and a Morphological Disambiguator for Kazakh Language. *Linguistics and Literature Studies*, 4(1):96–104.

[Lindén et al.2011] Krister Lindén, Erik Axelson, Sam Hardwick, Miikka Silfverberg, and Tommi Pirinen. 2011. HFST–framework for compiling and applying morphologies. pages 67–85.

[Oflazer1994] Kemal Oflazer. 1994. Two-level description of turkish morphology. *Literary and Linguistic Computing,*, 9(2):137–148.

[Orhun et al.2009] Murat Orhun, A. Cüneyd Tantug, and Esref Adali. 2009. Rule based analysis of the uyghur nouns. *Int. J. of Asian Lang. Proc.*, 19(1):33–44.

[Şahin et al.2013] Muhammet Şahin, Umut Sulubacak, and Gülşen Eryiğit. 2013. Redefinition of turkish morphology using flag diacritics. In *Proceedings of The Tenth Symposium on Natural Language Processing (SNLP-2013)*, Phuket, Thailand, October.

[Tantug et al.2006] A Cüneyd Tantug, Esref Adali, and Kemal Oflazer. 2006. Computer Analysis of the Turkmen Language Morphology. *FinTAL*, 4139:186–193.

A   Supplemental Material

We provide the diagrams for the full FST's as supplementary material.

The supplementary materials are available at
```
http://www2.isikun.edu.tr/
personel/ercan.solak/MorAz/index.
html
```

Evaluation of Finite State Morphological Analyzers Based on Paradigm Extraction from Wiktionary

Ling Liu and **Mans Hulden**
Department of Linguistics
University of Colorado
`first.last@colorado.edu`

Abstract

Wiktionary provides lexical information for an increasing number of languages, including morphological inflection tables. It is a good resource for automatically learning rule-based analysis of the inflectional morphology of a language. This paper performs an extensive evaluation of a method to extract generalized paradigms from morphological inflection tables, which can be converted to weighted and unweighted finite transducers for morphological parsing and generation. The inflection tables of 55 languages from the English edition of Wiktionary are converted to such general paradigms, and the performance of the probabilistic parsers based on these paradigms are tested.

1 Introduction

Morphological inflection is used in many languages to convey syntactic and semantic information. It is a systematic source of sparsity for NLP tasks, especially for languages with rich morphological systems where one lexeme can be inflected into as many as over a million distinct word forms (Kibrik, 1998). In this case, morphological parsers which can convert the inflected word forms back to the lemma forms, or the other way around can largely benefit downstream tasks, like part-of-speech tagging, language modeling, and machine translation (Tseng et al., 2005; Hulden and Francom, 2012; Duh and Kirchhoff, 2004; Avramidis and Koehn, 2008). Various approaches have been adopted to tackle the morphological inflection and lemmatization problem. For example, Durrett and DeNero (2013) automatically extracts transformation rules from labeled data and learns how to apply these rules with a discriminative sequence model. Kann and Schütze (2016) proposes to use a recurrent neural network (RNN) encoder-decoder model to generate an inflected form of a lemma for a target morphological tag combination. The SIGMORPHON 2016 shared task (Cotterell et al., 2016) of morphological reinflection received 11 systems which used various approaches such as conditional random fields (CRF), RNNs, and other linguistics-inspired heuristics. Among all the methods, one standard technology is to use finite-state transducers, which are more interpretable and manually modifiable, and thus more easily incorporated into and made to assist linguists' work. Hulden (2014) presents a method to generalize inflection tables into paradigms with finite state implementations and Forsberg and Hulden (2016) subsequently introduce how to transform morphological inflection tables into both unweighted and weighted finite transducers and apply the transducers to parsing and generation, the result of which is very promising, especially for facilitating and assisting linguists' work in addition to applications to morphological parsing and generation for downstream NLP tasks. However, the system was evaluated with only three languages (German, Spanish, and Finnish), all with Latin script. This paper intends to carry out a more extensive evaluation of this method.

Wiktionary[1] provides a source of morphological paradigms for a wide and still increasing range of languages, which is a useful resource of crosslinguistic research. The data in this work also originate with Wiktionary.

In this paper we evaluate the cross-linguistic performance of the paradigm generalization method on 55 languages, of which inflection tables have been extracted from the Wiktionary data. All the languages are consistently annotated with universal morphological tags (Sylak-Glassman et al., 2015) and are in the native orthography. In particular, we evaluate the accuracy on the ability to lemmatize previously unseen word forms and the

---

[1] http://www.wiktionary.org

Proceedings of the 13th International Conference on Finite State Methods and Natural Language Processing, pages 69–74,
Umeå, Sweden, 4–6 September 2017. © 2017 Association for Computational Linguistics
https://doi.org/10.18653/v1/W17-4009

inflection table	LCS = **schrib**	"paradigm"
schrei ben	x_1 = **schr**	x_1+**e**+x_2+x_3+**en**
schrei bend	x_2 = **i**	x_1+**e**+x_2+x_3+**end**
geschr ieben	x_3 = **b**	**ge**+x_1+x_2+**e**+x_3+**en**
schrei be	$\longrightarrow$	x_1+**e**+x_2+x_3+**e**
schrei b st		x_1+**e**+x_2+x_3+**st**
schrei b t		x_1+**e**+x_2+x_3+**t**
x_1 x_2 x_3		

Figure 1: Illustration of the paradigm extraction mechanism. An inflection table is given as input, and the longest common subsequence (LCS) is extracted and assigned to "variable parts" of a more abstract paradigm, based on discontinuities in the LCS. Several inflection tables may yield the same "paradigm" in which case paradigms are collapsed, and information about the shape of the variable strings x_i is retained for statistical modeling.

ability to assign correct morphosyntactic tags to a word form.

2   Paradigm Extraction

The paradigm extraction method is based on the idea of finding, among a list of related word forms, the longest common subsequence (LCS) shared by the forms. After the extraction, the LCS is marked in each word form and assigned to "paradigm variables". These variables are parts that are mutable in a paradigm, i.e. may change when going from one lemma to another, while the remaining, non-variable parts represent inflectional information. Figure 1 illustrates this process by showing a few forms of the German verb **schreiben**, the extraction of the LCS, and the assignment of the LCS into variable parts.

After such a generalization process, many paradigm representations which were generated from inflection tables turn out to be identical— indicating that the participating lemmas inflect according to the same pattern. Identical paradigms are collapsed, and the information about what strings were witnessed in the variable slots is stored for creating a probabilistic model of inflection. The reader is referred to (Hulden, 2014; Ahlberg et al., 2014; Ahlberg et al., 2015) for details.

This model already provides a method for performing morphological analysis when previously unseen word forms are encountered. One can create a transducer based on the paradigms that maps entries in a paradigm back to their lemma form in such a way that the variable parts x_i may correspond to any arbitrary string. For example, the paradigm in figure 1 would yield a lemmatizing transducer that would map e.g. **geliehen**

$\mapsto$ **leihen** since the **l** can be assumed to match the variable x_1, the **i** x_2, and the **h** x_3. Forsberg and Hulden (2016) developl a model that creates such lemmatizing transducers from inflection tables, which also return the inflectional information of the source word form.

2.1   Analyzing word forms

This model has the disadvantage of often returning a large number of plausible analyses due to the fact that an unseen word form may fit many different learned paradigms, and also fit them in many different slots. One can, however, induce a language model of each variable part x_i in the paradigms and create a probabilistic model which favors production of such analyses where variable parts resemble those that have been seen in the training data. An n-gram model over the variables seen in each paradigm can be formulated as follows. Many paradigms have been collapsed from a large number of inflection tables which provide us with statistics over the shape of the x_i parts. We can, when trying to fit an unseen word form with a variable x_i consisting of letters $v_1, \ldots v_n$ into a paradigm and slot to produce its lemma, calculate the joint probability using an n-gram approximation of the letters according to the expression:

$$P(v_1, \ldots, v_n) = \prod_{i=1}^{n} P(v_i | v_{i-(n-1)}, \ldots, v_{i-1}) \tag{1}$$

These quantities can be estimated by maximum likelihood from the the training data as:

$$P(v_i | v_{i-(n-1)}, \ldots, v_{i-1})$$
$$= \frac{\#(v_{i-(n-1)}, \ldots, v_{i-1}, v_i)}{\#(v_{i-(n-1)}, \ldots, v_{i-1})} \tag{2}$$

Such a model is induced for each variable $x_1, \ldots, x_n$ in a paradigm, and when a proposed analysis is evaluated, the quantity $p(x_i, \ldots, x_n) = p(x_1) \times \ldots \times p(x_n)$ is evaluated to give a score of fit of a proposed variable assignment for a word to be analyzed.

For example, to calculate the fit of **geliehen** into the slot **ge**+x_1+x_2+**e**+x_3+**en** (Figure 1), we would evaluate $p(x_1) = $ **l**, $p(x_2) = $ **i** and $p(x_3) = $ **h** based on the above, yielding a probability estimate of the slot and paradigm matching the word form **geliehen**. Likewise, every possible assignment of variable parts in every paradigm will be calculated. This process can be encoded into a weighted finite state transducer (WFST) following Forsberg and Hulden (2016).

Language	Language group	Script
Adyghe	Northwest Caucasian	Cyrillic
Albanian	IE other	Latin (Albanian alphabet)
Armenian	IE other	Armenian
Asturian	IE/Italic/Romance/Western	Latin
Bashkir	Turkic	Cyrillic, Latin, Arabic
Basque	Language Isolate	Latin (Basque alphabet)
Bengali	IE/Indo-Iranian/Indo-Aryan	Eastern Nagari script (Bengali alphabet)
Bulgarian	IE/Balto-Slavic/Slavic	Cyrillic (Bulgarian alphabet)
Catalan	IE/Italic/Romance/Western	Latin (Catalan alphabet)
Danish	IE/Germanic/North G	Latin (Dano-Norwegian alphabet)
Dutch	IE/Germanic/West G	Latin (Dutch alphabet)
Esperanto	Created	Latin (Esperanto alphabet)
Estonian	Uralic/Finnic	Latin (Estonian alphabet)
Faroese	IE/Germanic/North G	Latin (Faroese orthography)
Finnish	Uralic/Finnic	Latin (Finnish alphabet)
French	IE/Italic/Romance/Western	Latin (French alphabet)
Friulian	IE/Italic/Romance/Western	Latin
Galician	IE/Italic/Romance/Western	Latin (Galician alphabet)
Georgian	Kartvelian	Georgian
German	IE/Germanic/West G	Latin (German alphabet)
Greek	IE/Hellenic	Greek
Hebrew	Afro-Asiatic/Semitic/Central S	Hebrew
Hindi	IE/Indo-Iranian/Indo-Aryan	Devanagari
Hungarian	Uralic/Finno-Ugric	Latin (Hungarian alphabet)
Icelandic	IE/Germanic/North G	Latin (Icelandic alphabet)
Italian	IE/Italic/Romance/Italo-Dalmatian	Latin (Italian alphabet)
Ladin	IE/Italic/Romance/Western	Latin
Latin	IE/Italic/Latino-Faliscan	Latin
Latvian	IE/Balto-Slavic/Baltic	Latin (Latvian alphabet)
Lithuanian	IE/Balto-Slavic/Baltic	Latin (Lithuanian alphabet)
Lower Sorbian	IE/Balto-Slavic/Slavic/West S	Latin (Sorbian alphabet)
Luxembourgish	IE/Germanic/West G	Latin (Luxembourgish alphabet)
Macedonian	IE/Balto-Slavic/Slavic/South S	Cyrillic (Macedonian alphabet)
Navajo	Da-Dene/Athabaskan	Latin
Northern Sami	Uralic/Sami	Latin (Northern Sami alphabet)
Norwegian Bokmal	IE/Germanic/North G	Latin (Norwegian alphabet)
Norwegian Nynorsk	IE/Germanic/North G	Latin (Norwegian alphabet)
Occitan	IE/Italic/Romance/Gallo-R	Latin
Polish	IE/Balto-Slavic/Slavic/West S	Latin (Polish alphabet)
Portuguese	IE/Italic/Romance/Western R	Latin (Portuguese alphabet)
Quechua	Quechua	Latin (Quechua alphabet)
Romanian	IE/Italic/Romance/Eastern R	Latin (Romanian alphabet)
Russian	IE/Balto-Slavic/Slavic/East S	Cyrillic (Russian alphabet)
Sanskrit	IE/Indo-Iranian/Indo-Aryan	Brahmic
Scottish Gaelic	IE/Celtic	Latin (Scottish Gaelic orthography)
Slovak	IE/Balto-Slavic/Slavic/West S	Latin (Slovak alphabet)
Slovene	IE/Balto-Slavic/Slavic/South S	Latin (Slovene alphabet)
Spanish	IE/Italic/Romance/Western	Latin (Spanish alphabet)
Swahili	Niger-Congo	Latin (Roman Swahili alphabet)
Swedish	IE/Germanic/North G	Latin (Swedish alphabet)
Turkish	Turkic	Latin (Turkish alphabet)
Ukrainian	IE/Balto-Slavic/Slavic/East	Cyrillic (Ukrainian alphabet)
Urdu	IE/Indo-Iranian/Indo-Aryan	Extended Perso-Arabic (Urdu alphabet)
Venetian	IE/Italic/Romance/Italo-Western	Latin
Welsh	IE/Celtic	Latin (Welsh alphabet)

Table 1: Languages, Language Groups, and Scripts

2.2 Evaluation

The paradigm extraction and application method presented in the previous part is evaluated with 55 languages from the Wiktionary Morphological Database[2] (Kirov et al., 2016) as part of the UniMorph project[3] which includes data for 350 languages at the time we downloaded it.[4] For each of the 55 languages, we learn paradigms from a random selection of 90% of the available inflection tables and leave 10% of the tables as held-out data. Tables for different parts-of-speech are generalized identically and the system does not keep these separate (although it is unlikely that a noun would inflect like a verb, for example). This means that the POS information is treated as a normal tag and we may receive analyses with different parts of speech.

The evaluation task is to convert the inflected word form back to its lemma form and assign it morphological tags. At test time, we analyze each form in the held-out tables separately and evaluate the accuracy on the highest scoring analysis. We report accuracies on several combinations of lemmatization correctness, morphosyntactic tag correctness and POS tag correctness.

The 55 languages fall into 19 language groups: Caucasian, Indo-European other, Italic (Romance, with the exception of Latin), Turkic, Language isolated, Indo-Aryan, Slavic, Baltic, Germanic, Uralic, Celtic, Semitic, Hellenic, Kartvelian, Da-Dene, Quechua, Turkic, Niger-Congo, and an artificial language—Esperanto. The data for each language is in its native script, which consists of 10 different scripts: Latin, Cyrillic, Armenian, Eastern Nagari, Georgian, Greek, Hebrew, Devanagari, Brahmic, and Pero-Arabic. The criterion for selecting the 55 languages is that each language has 8,000 or more entries in the original data in UniMorph Wiktionary Morphological Database. Languages with less entries are selected to increase the representativeness of the data. A summary of the languages, language groups and scripts is presented in table 1. The data for each language is used just at it is from the database. Little work is done to improve the quality of the data. Therefore, if there are misspellings or incorrect inflections in the data set, the paradigms are extracted and tested with any errors uncorrected.

The number of inflection tables may not be the same as the number of lemmas, because in cases where there are alternative inflected forms for one morphosyntactic description of a lemma in the UniMorph database, each form is represented in a separate table.

---

[2]https://github.com/ckirov/UniMorph/tree/master/data

[3]http://www.unimorph.org

[4]The 55 languages are: Adyghe, Albanian, Armenian, Asturian, Bashkir, Basque, Bengali, Bulgarian, Catalan, Danish, Dutch, Esperanto, Estonian, Faroese, Finnish, French, Friulian, Galician, Georgian, German, Greek, Hebrew, Hindi, Hungarian, Icelandic, Italian, Ladin, Latin, Latvian, Lithuanian, Lower Sorbian, Luxembourgish, Macedonian, Navajo, Northern Sami, Norwegian, Bokmal, Norwegian Nynorsk, Occitan, Polish, Portuguese, Quechua, Romanian, Russian, Sanskrit, Scottish Gaelic, Slovak, Slovene, Spanish, Swahili, Swedish, Turkish, Ukrainian, Urdu, Venetian, Welsh.

Language	LT	LPOS	LEMMA	TNum	PAllNum	P1Ex	P2Ex	PMEx	P0Var	TopFreq	WNum	LNum
Adyghe	0.6012	0.6012	0.7887	1,593	16	5	1	10	0	550	18,874	1,593
Albanian	0.7016	0.7100	0.7179	616	68	36	6	21	5	121	37,411	589
Armenian	0.8994	0.9010	0.9631	14,905	305	104	32	158	11	1,730	703,902	7,040
Asturian	0.8840	0.8933	0.9140	1,304	113	58	14	39	2	235	41,835	938
Bashkir	0.8816	0.9245	0.9245	773	36	6	2	28	0	92	8,981	773
Basque	0.0	0.0	0.0021	45	44	38	0	0	6	1	13,627	45
Basque2	0.1276	0.3111	0.3588	620	504	9	0	2	493	52	27788	620
Bengali	0.7234	0.7255	0.7255	225	74	55	3	15	1	21	5,691	136
Bulgarian	0.7429	0.7445	0.7627	2,912	225	98	25	96	6	315	55,523	2,471
Catalan	0.8550	0.8894	0.8894	1,558	107	59	11	33	4	779	83,182	1,557
Danish	0.6826	0.6945	0.7075	3,180	248	180	11	57	0	658	28,584	3,180
Dutch	0.6993	0.7110	0.7323	4,985	274	112	34	128	0	959	60,437	4,979
Esperanto	0.7628	0.7638	0.7700	23,687	46	28	2	13	3	11,652	98,565	23,687
Estonian	0.5958	0.5970	0.5970	887	779	776	2	1	0	19	39,102	886
Faroese	0.5121	0.5297	0.5702	3,333	621	419	62	135	5	217	52,836	3,077
Finnish	0.6803	0.6823	0.7633	20,000	2,403	862	477	1,064	0	685	627,085	14,274
French	0.7412	0.7466	0.8556	19,937	1,248	604	201	428	15	2,241	387,669	7,555
Friulian	0.7844	0.7844	0.7929	155	37	22	2	8	5	73	6,593	145
Galician	0.7389	0.7485	0.7613	486	63	32	7	22	2	184	29,843	472
Georgian	0.6623	0.6630	0.7828	3,784	63	49	3	11	0	2,117	78,196	3,782
German	0.6221	0.6510	0.8216	17,749	851	512	100	239	0	1653	197,080	15,059
Greek	0.6555	0.6619	0.6938	9,861	2,072	1,426	212	377	57	468	149,187	8,780
Hebrew	0.8217	0.8263	0.8288	867	555	437	58	55	4	9	24,247	510
Hindi	0.9692	0.9696	0.9746	852	33	10	6	16	1	184	72,424	788
Hindi2	0.9522	0.9553	0.9597	788	31	11	4	15	1	181	58,856	788
Hungarian	0.8550	0.9197	0.9277	15,838	4,136	3,640	37	173	286	1,009	597,744	13,952
Icelandic	0.6917	0.7158	0.7233	5,082	384	155	46	170	14	377	86,864	4,769
Italian	0.8972	0.8973	0.8973	10,009	374	238	32	98	6	3919	519,571	10,009
Ladin	0.8400	0.8595	0.8875	813	111	72	11	20	8	97	17,830	512
Latin	0.8155	0.8167	0.8406	25,079	2,463	1,602	275	567	19	3,643	967,062	20,497
Latvian	0.7943	0.8269	0.8450	10,067	519	275	66	167	11	1,722	216,420	7,558
Lithuanian	0.7786	0.7820	0.7969	1,925	515	298	79	133	5	130	58,814	1,458
Lower Sorbian	0.6098	0.6265	0.6273	1,224	351	260	18	70	3	57	25,062	994
Luxembourgish	0.7422	0.7554	0.7591	1,277	222	172	12	34	4	318	48,175	1,276
Macedonian	0.7319	0.7563	0.7837	10,313	272	134	16	114	8	869	178,363	10,310
Navajo	0.2649	0.2746	0.2912	675	455	398	22	17	18	61	13,059	674
N Sami	0.4377	0.4414	0.4476	2,203	1,343	1,250	41	52	0	44	66,344	2,107
N Bokmal	0.5866	0.6170	0.6733	5,750	355	211	42	99	3	1,097	24,704	5,518
N Nynorsk	0.5959	0.6242	0.6720	5,041	380	237	44	94	5	1,333	23,093	4,677
Occitan	0.9474	0.9474	0.9555	173	28	19	3	6	0	101	5,162	172
Polish	0.6967	0.7059	0.7138	10,698	1,300	737	161	398	4	566	202,927	10,179
Portuguese	0.9053	0.9062	0.9369	5,088	283	162	11	107	3	2,400	309,084	4,001
Quechua	0.4513	0.4515	0.9128	1,244	17	8	0	9	0	372	181,248	1,006
Romanian	0.6258	0.6380	0.6989	3,504	671	447	76	144	4	205	68,174	3,479
Russian	0.7100	0.7615	0.7749	28,017	1,669	825	231	612	1	1,898	460,981	27,924
Sanskrit	0.6847	0.7029	0.7998	924	79	43	7	26	3	243	27,031	924
S Gaelic	0.9231	0.9692	0.9692	101	74	61	9	3	1	4	1,208	70
Slovak	0.5582	0.5899	0.5912	1,093	250	137	42	68	3	116	16,435	1,046
Slovene	0.4383	0.4646	0.4886	2,601	949	747	62	115	25	150	64,504	2,554
Spanish	0.9037	0.9038	0.9355	6,355	420	194	52	169	5	1,977	389,308	5,460
Swahili	0.8550	0.8559	0.8567	74	42	40	0	2	0	20	12,365	74
Swedish	0.6928	0.7156	0.7615	10,833	458	243	57	155	4	1,188	92,890	10,503
Turkish	0.8286	0.8414	0.8480	3,572	237	97	29	111	0	155	278,624	3,572
Ukrainian	0.5645	0.5900	0.5948	1,494	248	155	30	62	3	142	22,398	1,493
Urdu	0.8784	0.8827	0.8827	182	51	43	1	7	0	40	12,755	182
Venetian	0.8160	0.8342	0.9327	959	112	73	10	22	7	193	29,790	607
Welsh	0.2378	0.2478	0.2478	183	158	155	1	2	1	4	10824	183

Table 2: Result Summary. LT–Lemma+Tags, LPOS–Lemma+POS, LEMMA–Lemma, TNum–The number of inflection tables in the data, PAllNum–The number of all paradigms for each language, P1Ex–The number of paradigms with only 1 example for the variable(s), P2Ex–The number of paradigms with only 2 examples for the variable(s), PMEx–The number of paradigms with more than 2 examples for the variable(s), P0Var–The number of paradigms with no variable in it, TopFreq – The number of examples for the most popular paradigm, WNum–The number of words, LNum–The number of lemmas, N Sami–Northern Sami, N Bokmal–Norwegian Bokmal, N Nynorsk–Norwegian Nynorsk, S Gaelic–Scottish Gaelic, Basque2–result of Basque with more data, Hindi2–result of Hindi without alternative inflections

3   Result and Discussion

More abstract paradigms are extracted successfully from all the morphological tables in the training set for each of the 55 languages. Lemmatization correctness ranges from a low end of 0% (Basque) to a high end of 96.3% (Armenian), 97.5% (Hindi). The lemma-POS accuracy ranges from 0% (Basque) to 97.0% (Hindi). The joint lemma-tag accuracy ranges from 0% (Basque) to 96.9% (Hindi).

One advantage of the probabilistic model is that it can rank the parsing and generation through the language model over variables. For the evaluation, we use only the most likely one. However, there can still be alternatives for the top ranking result. For example, the French word **écris** gets five analyses: **[écrir V; IND; PRS; 1; SG]**, **[écrir V; IND; PRS; 2; SG]**, **[écrir V; IND; PST; 1; SG; PFV]**, **[écrir V; IND; PST; 2; SG; PFV]** and **[écrir V; POS; IMP; 2; SG]**, with the same lemma form and part-of-speech, but different tags. We evaluate the recall of the lemma and all tags, lemma and only part-of-speech, and only lemma. Table 2 presents a summary of the evaluation result, as well as the data size for each language in terms of word counts, lemma counts and table counts, the number of abstract paradigms extracted for each language, the paradigm distribution as to their instantiation case numbers, and the number of instances for the most popular paradigm.

The results seem to correlate strongly with the amount of available data. For languages where only a few inflection tables are seen, or where all inflection tables represent the same paradigm, accuracies are low. For example, the initial evaluation on Basque is only 45 lemmas (and the number of inflection tables is the same), with 44 as training and 1 held-out for test. Each of the inflection table represents a distinct paradigm as is reflected by the fact that the number of abstract paradigms is the same as the training data size, i.e. 44. Therefore, the result of Basque is very low. A second round of evaluation was conducted with more data and the result is added to Table 2 as Basque2. The increased Basque data is 620 lemmas, with 558 used for training and 62 for testing. The result is still low but better than the initial one, because the paradigms become more representative with a larger coverage, which is testified by the most representative paradigm getting 52 instantiations from the training data. The result of Navajo is close to that of Basque2. The data sizes of the two languages are similar (Basque2 620, Navajo 675). For Navajo, the number of paradigms is 455, and for Basque2, the number of paradigms is 504. Basque2 has 493 paradigms without variables (i.e. 493 paradigms with only one instantiations), and Navajo has 398 paradigms with only one instantiation in the training data. The similarity of the results coincides with the fact that both languages are morphologically complex, and Basque morphology has even more variation. Conversely, languages where many different types of inflection tables are seen and the inflection tables are representative of the language morphology (reflected in a higher paradigm count and a lower ratio of paradigm counts to table counts), produce analyzers that can perform quite robustly. For example, the Hindi data produces 33 paradigms out of the 767 inflection training tables, resulting in a coverage where the recall for each of the three tests is over 95%. As alternative inflections of a lemma are represented with different tables, the recall may be higher than the case where each lemma gets only one inflection table, i.e. where no related form of the associated lemma has been witnessed. However, as alternative inflections are limited, keeping them with different tables should not influence the result by a large extent. Hindi2 is the result for Hindi using only one inflection table for each lemma and ignoring alternative inflections.

4   Conclusion

Generalized paradigms are successfully extracted for all the 55 languages from 19 language groups in 10 different scripts. For languages with a large size of representative data, the recalls of the lemma, lemma plus part-of-speech, and lemma plus all tags can be as high as over 95%. However, for languages for which the data is limited or less representative, the recalls are very low. This indicates that the method to extract generalized paradigms from morphological inflection tables works well despite linguistic diversity and script variations. The probabilistic model can yield good predictions and analyses when the available data for a language is sufficient and representative.

Acknowledgements

This work has been partly sponsored by DARPA I20 in the LORELEI program.

References

Malin Ahlberg, Markus Forsberg, and Mans Hulden. 2014. Semi-supervised learning of morphological paradigms and lexicons. In *Proceedings of the 14th Conference of the European Chapter of the Association for Computational Linguistics*, pages 569–578, Gothenburg, Sweden. Association for Computational Linguistics.

Malin Ahlberg, Markus Forsberg, and Mans Hulden. 2015. Paradigm classification in supervised learning of morphology. In *Proceedings of the 2015 Conference of the North American Chapter of the Association for Computational Linguistics: Human Language Technologies*, pages 1024–1029, Denver, Colorado, May–June. Association for Computational Linguistics.

Eleftherios Avramidis and Philipp Koehn. 2008. Enriching morphologically poor languages for statistical machine translation. In *ACL*, pages 763–770.

Ryan Cotterell, Christo Kirov, John Sylak-Glassman, David Yarowsky, Jason Eisner, and Mans Hulden. 2016. The SIGMORPHON 2016 shared task—morphological reinflection. *ACL 2016*, page 10.

Kevin Duh and Katrin Kirchhoff. 2004. Automatic learning of language model structure. In *Proceedings of the 20th international conference on Computational Linguistics*, page 148. Association for Computational Linguistics.

Greg Durrett and John DeNero. 2013. Supervised learning of complete morphological paradigms. In *HLT-NAACL*, pages 1185–1195.

Markus Forsberg and Mans Hulden. 2016. Learning transducer models for morphological analysis from example inflections. *ACL 2016*, page 42.

Mans Hulden and Jerid Francom. 2012. Boosting statistical tagger accuracy with simple rule-based grammars. In *LREC*, pages 2114–2117.

Mans Hulden. 2014. Generalizing inflection tables into paradigms with finite state operations. In *Proceedings of the 2014 Joint Meeting of SIGMORPHON and SIGFSM*, pages 29–36.

Katharina Kann and Hinrich Schütze. 2016. Single-model encoder-decoder with explicit morphological representation for reinflection. *arXiv preprint arXiv:1606.00589*.

Aleksandr E. Kibrik. 1998. Archi. In Andrew Spencer and Arnold M. Zwicky, editors, *The Handbook of Morphology*, pages 455–476. Oxford: Blackwell Publishers.

Christo Kirov, John Sylak-Glassman, Roger Que, and David Yarowsky. 2016. Very-large scale parsing and normalization of wiktionary morphological paradigms. In *Proceedings of the Tenth International Conference on Language Resources and Evaluation (LREC 2016)*, pages 3121–3126.

John Sylak-Glassman, Christo Kirov, Matt Post, Roger Que, and David Yarowsky. 2015. A universal feature schema for rich morphological annotation and fine-grained cross-lingual part-of-speech tagging. In Cerstin Mahlow and Michael Piotrowski, editors, *Proceedings of the 4th Workshop on Systems and Frameworks for Computational Morphology (SFCM)*, pages 72–93. Springer, Berlin.

Huihsin Tseng, Daniel Jurafsky, and Christopher Manning. 2005. Morphological features help POS tagging of unknown words across language varieties. In *Proceedings of the fourth SIGHAN workshop on Chinese language processing*, pages 32–39.

Evaluating an Automata Approach to Query Containment

Michael Minock

KTH Royal Institute of Technology, Stockholm, Sweden
Umeå University, Umeå, Sweden.
`minock@kth.se, mjm@cs.umu.se`

Abstract

Given two queries Q_{super} and Q_{sub}, query containment is the problem of determining if $Q_{sub}(D) \subseteq Q_{super}(D)$ for all databases D. This problem has long been explored, but to our knowledge no one has empirically evaluated a straightforward application of finite state automata to the problem. We do so here, covering the case of conjunctive queries with limited set conditions. We evaluate an implementation of our approach against straightforward implementations of both the canonical database and theorem proving approaches. Our implementation outperforms theorem proving on a natural language interface corpus over a photo/video domain. It also outperforms the canonical database implementation on single relation queries with large set conditions.

1 Introduction

Given the queries Q_{super} and Q_{sub}, *query containment* is the problem of determining if $Q_{sub}(D) \subseteq Q_{super}(D)$ for all databases D. Not only interesting in itself, the problem is of practical importance in query optimization, data integration (Ullman, 2000) and, of note here, in natural language generation (Shieber, 1993), dialogue (Bos and Oka, 2002) and understanding (Minock, 2017).

Over time, increasingly complex cases of the problem have been solved: relational conjunctive queries (Chandra and Merlin, 1977); conjunctive queries with arithmetic comparisons over dense domains (Klug, 1988); negation of subgoals (Levy, 1999). More recent work[1] has looked at the problem for queries with aggregate operators (see the survey (Cohen, 2005)). Remarkably, the decidability of the problem remains open for queries under bag semantics (Afrati et al., 2010).

A typical approach to solving query containment is to generate a *canonical database* D' that represents Q_{sub} and then to evaluate $Q_{super}(D')$. If the answer to Q_{sub} within D' is within $Q_{super}(D')$, then Q_{super} contains Q_{sub} (see (Ullman, 2000)). Another approach to solve the problem is via *theorem proving*. If ϕ is the translation of Q_{super} to a first order formula free over the answer variables of Q_{super}, and likewise φ for Q_{sub}, then, assuming that the queries are compatible (i.e. $free(\phi) = free(\varphi)$), $\neg\mathsf{SAT}(\exists free(\phi)(\neg\phi \wedge \varphi))$ if and only if Q_{super} contains Q_{sub}. A third approach, and what we look at here, is to use reduce query containment to determining the if a finite state automaton recognizes the empty language. Here we present, implement, and empirically evaluate such an approach. We compare performance against a canonical database and theorem proving implementation over a photo/video querying corpus. We also conduct several special scalability tests for queries with many predicates over the same relation and queries with large set conditions over a single relation.

2 Preliminaries

As is common, we present queries here in DATA-LOG, with which we assume the reader is familiar (see (Ullman, 1988)). As a quick refresher, under the database state and queries of Figure 1, the answer to Q1 is `{(h), (i)}` and the answer to Q2 is `{(h)}`. In fact no matter what the state of the database is, answers of Q2 are always contained in the answers of Q1. Likewise, Q3 contains Q1.

Before continuing, it is worth giving example runs of the canonical database and theorem prov-

---

[1]The problem has also been addressed in semi-structured query languages (Baumgartner et al., 2005; Björklund et al., 2011) and in description logics (Baader et al., 2009). Still the focus here is on query containment for relational databases.

Proceedings of the 13th International Conference on Finite State Methods and Natural Language Processing, pages 75–79,
Umeå, Sweden, 4–6 September 2017. © 2017 Association for Computational Linguistics
https://doi.org/10.18653/v1/W17-4010

```
R(A, B, C)    S(D, E)    T(F G)
  h  i  j       h  r
  i  k  l       i  b
  j  m  n       j  b
                k  r

Q1(X)  :- R(X,Y,Z), S(Y,P)
Q2(X)  :- R(X,Y,Z), S(Y,'b'), S(Z,'b')
Q3(X)  :- R(X,Y,Z)
```

Figure 1: Example database state and queries.

ing approaches for deciding whether Q1 contains Q2. Under the canonical database approach, each variable in Q_{sub} (i.e. Q2) generates a fresh constant (we use the natural numbers). Predicates in the body of the conjunctive query Q_{sub} are frozen with these constants and generate tuples in the canonical database. Thus the canonical database state for Q2 is $\{R(1,2,3),S(2,'b'),S(3,'b')\}$ with the frozen answer being $\{(1)\}$. It is easy to verify that Q1 evaluated over this database state, generates the frozen answer and thus Q1 contains Q2. In the theorem proving approach, the sentence sent to the SAT solver is $(\exists x)(\neg(\exists y, z, p)(R(x,y,z) \wedge S(y,p)) \wedge (\exists y, z, p1, p2)(R(x,y,z) \wedge S(y,p1) \wedge S(y,p2) \wedge p1 = 'b' \wedge p2 = 'b'))$. We now turn to our finite state automata approach.

3 An Automata-based Approach

The approach we develop here is quite straightforward. In short, for a query Q, we build the automaton M_Q which recognizes the language of database state encodings which generate non-empty answers to Q. Given the closure properties of regular languages, the query containment problem reduces to determining if $L(\overline{M_{Q_{super}}}) \cap L(M_{Q_{sub}})$ is empty.

Under simple runs of building M_Q, the resulting automaton is linear with a single final state. More complex runs require branching over variable settings, resulting in a tree shaped automaton with multiple final states. In general post processing is required to bypass parts of the automaton for which a witnessing tuple have already been consumed. Finally an assumption that tuples appear in a fixed lexicographic order compresses the automaton. The remainder of the section presents our approach in greater detail.

3.1 Encoding Database States

By way of example, the database state in Figure 1 is encoded as `hij_ikl_jmn_#hr_ib_jb_kr_##`. We are using the symbol _ to close off tuples and

the symbol # to close off relation states. An *encoding scheme* orders a finite set of relations (and their attributes) and specifies which constants may appear under which attributes.

3.2 Fixing a Minimal Encoding Scheme

When deciding if Q_{super} contains Q_{sub}, we fix a minimal encoding scheme that covers both queries. First we collect the relations used in the bodies of both queries and, for efficiency, truncate these relations to include only the attributes used in join conditions, simple conditions or the head of a query. For example, in the containment problem determining if Q3 contains Q1, R is truncated down to two attributes. Given this we then determine an arbitrary ordering over the truncated relations. To add constants under variables, reminiscent of the canonical database approach, variables and constants of Q_{sub} are frozen and added as constants (e.g. X becomes 'x', and 'b' remains 'b') under their corresponding attributes.

For example, for the problem if Q1 contains Q2, we collect the database relations R and S. Neither may be truncated. Arbitrarily we determine the relation ordering to be [R, S]. The constants under the attributes are 'x' under A, 'y' under B, 'z' under C, 'y' and 'z' under D and 'b' under E.

3.3 Building the Automaton M_Q

Given a query Q and an encoding scheme, we truncate and sort the predicates in the body of Q based on the encoding scheme. We then walk the new truncated/sorted query body from left to right constructing an automaton as we go. For each relation in the encoding, we construct what we term a *relation gobbler*. These relation gobblers consume associated relations in the input database state expression. They are chained together using a transition on the symbol # from the last state of one gobbler to the first state of the next.

In the normal case, in which the relation appears in a predicate in the truncated/sorted query body, the relation gobbler consists of what we term a *tuple gobbler*, followed by a *witness gobbler*, followed by a *tuple gobbler*. Tuple gobblers nondeterministically consume irrelevant tuples. The witness gobbler recognizes a tuple that matches the current query predicate. In the case in which the relation name does not appear in a predicate of the truncated/sorted query[2], the relation gobbler

---

[2]This occurs because the relation name *does* appear in a

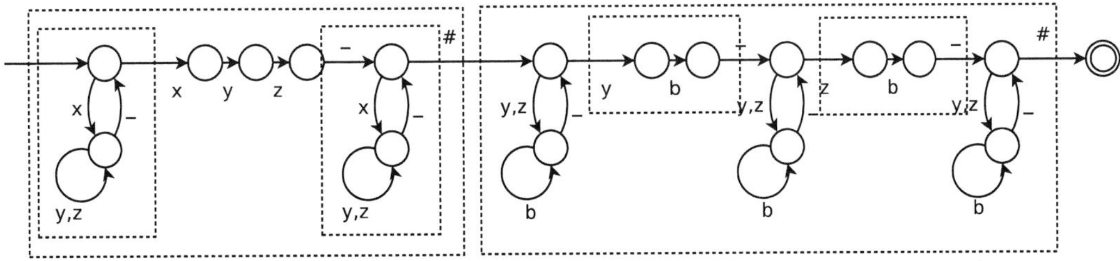

Figure 2: A NFA that recognizes a language that includes all encoded database states which generate answers to Q2 under the example encoding of 3.2, and no database state that does not generate answers.

consists of just a tuple gobbler. A special case occurs with predicates over the same relation name in a query. The relation gobbler for such cases is a chained sequence of tuple-witness-tuple gobblers.

The exact algorithm of this construction method is omitted here, but it is achieved via a fairly simple recursive function. Once the base case is reached, all the relations in the encoding have been treated and a final state after the last # is marked as accepting. The automaton in Figure 2 recognizes database states yielding answers to Q2 under the example encoding scheme in section 3.2. It consists of two relation gobblers, where the tuple gobblers are highlighted in the first and the witness gobbler in the second. Note that this automaton did not branch because there is only one constant under Y and only one constant under Z.

3.3.1 Branching on Variable Assignments

As we scan the predicates of the query body, a query variable may be bound to more than one constant. In such cases we branch the automaton to the alternative possibilities. For example, consider the encoding scheme of section 3.2, but with the relation ordering `[S,R]`. The automaton in Figure 3 shows the automaton (tuple gobblers are not expanded for reasons of space) that recognizes answers to Q2 under this alternative encoding scheme. This requires branching[3].

3.3.2 Witnesses over Multiple Predicates

When queries are self-joining (i.e. two or more predicates are over the same relation in the query body), the same tuple might need to serve as a witness in more than one witness gobbler. For example, consider the somewhat contrived `Q4(X) :- R(X,Y,Z),R(X,Y,Z)`. Clearly this is

---

predicate of the other query in the containment problem.

[3]In this particular case only one of the branches ultimately succeeds due to possible constants under attributes, but in general such branching can lead to multiple final states.

equivalent to `Q3(X)`. This is handled by walking the tree shaped (or linear) automaton, keeping track of which witnesses have been used so far. Any predicate gobbler that is already witnessed is bypassed and removed.

3.3.3 Ordered Database State Assumption

The arbitrary order in which witnesses might appear requires quite deep trees many of which check the same cases. We may invoke an assumption that witnesses may only appear in some given ordering in database states and easily enforce this in the recursive automata shortening routine of section 3.3.2. As will be shown, this can lead to considerable performance improvement.

3.4 The Containment Test

Given that the automaton for both Q_{super} and Q_{sub} are constructed over the same encoding scheme, we may construct an automaton that recognizes $L(\overline{M}_{Q_{super}}) \cap L(M_{Q_{sub}})$ which is empty when Q_{super} contains Q_{sub}.

4 Evaluation

Our approach (**FSA**) is implemented in Python and for most of its automata routines it uses PADS, a library of Python Algorithms and Data Structures implemented by David Eppstein of the University of California, Irvine. Although not described above, we extended FSA to handle limited set conditions. The current set conditions supported are set conditions on non-joining attributes over relations that appear in only one predicate of a query. We have also implemented Python versions of the canonical database (**CDB**) and the theorem proving (**TP**) approaches. The database system used in CDB is SQLITE running in main memory; performance deteriorates by several orders of magnitude if the database must be written to disk. Our CDB implementation is extended to set con-

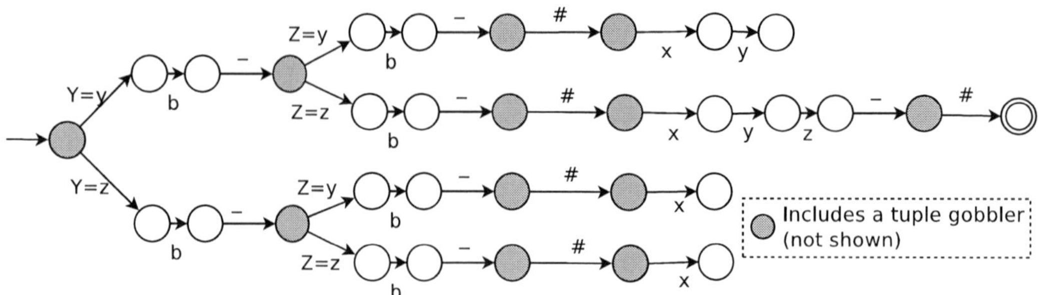

Figure 3: A NFA that recognizes Q2 under the relation ordering [S,R].

Approach	Avg	Max	Min
CDB	0.3	1.5	0.1
TP	11.3	33.8	7.6
FSA	1.9	23.6	0.1

Table 1: Results over photo/video corpus (ms)

Approach	Case 1	Case 2	Case 3
CDB	1.0	0.6	1703
TP	62009	64.3	56235
FSA	0.9	294.9	222

Table 2: Results for special cases (ms)

ditions by converting queries using set conditions into unions of (non-set) conjunctive queries. Each simple non set query in the conjunction is frozen and inserted into the same database state rather than the less efficient technique of building separate canonical databases for each combination. For TP, we use PROVER9.

We evaluate all three implementations using a corpus of natural language queries over a photo/video domain (available at sites.google.com/view/nli-corpora/). The corpus consists of a schema and a set of 100 natural language questions (e.g. "give photos of Alice with Bob in London in 2016".) paired with corresponding SQL queries. The portion of the corpus that we run our evaluation over are 27 queries over the Picture table restricted to conjunctive queries with simple and limited set conditions. Obviously CDB, TP and FSA each return the same containment determinations. Table 1 gives performance results over the $27 \times 27 = 729$ problems.

We also run a series of scalability tests to determine performance over long queries with multiple predicates over the same relation and queries with large set conditions on a single relation. To motivate, consider applications where arbitrary knowledge, constraints or complex view definitions are added to the query containment problem. Also consider cases where common names denote large sets or contexts sets are represented. To get insight into such cases, we measure performance of long queries over a single edge relation (case 1,2) and over large set conditions (case 3). Specifically the first case is exactly example one in (Chandra and Merlin, 1977) which gives a contrived query which, through reasoning, can be radically simplified. The second case, also derived from the same article, is based on reducing graph colorability of graph rings of length 9 and 10 are 2-colorable (False for 9, True for 10). Finally our third case is over a single relation of 5 attributes, where queries have set conditions over these attributes with between 7 and 14 distinct values. Table 2 shows results for these scalability tests.

In summary FSA performs reasonably well on the photo/video corpus and, in the case of large sets it performs better than CDB. TP performs the worst on the photo/video corpus and is dangerously vulnerable to blow up on the scalability cases 1 and 3. We view scalability case 1 as a *haphazard case* in which many predicates may be satisfied by the same witness. Case 2 is a *purposeful case* in which an NP-Complete problem is being constructed and separate witnesses are matched to each predicate. FSA does the poorest under case 2 and even worse (561 ms) if we remove the optimization of section 3.3.3. That said, we posit that case 1 is much more likely to fit real world problems in which database constraints and view definitions are added to containment problems. Thus we are not alarmed by FSA's relative weakness on case 2.

5   Discussion

It has long been recognized that natural language questions over databases require quite advanced semantics, going well beyond the simple conjunctive query case (Copestake and Jones, 1990). While we cover queries that use simple set conditions, enabling us to represent and/or ambiguities (e.g. *"photos of Alice and Bob"*), we still do not yet cover questions expressing point inequalities (e.g. *"photos of Alice not taken on June 1,2017"*), sub-goal negation (e.g. *"photos of Alice without Bob"*), superlatives (e.g. *"latest photo of Alice with Bob"*, cardinality conditions (e.g. *"who appears in the most pictures?"*) or non-recursive DATALOG with negated sub-goals (e.g. *"is Bob in every picture in London in 2016?"*, etc. These and many other hard examples appear in our photo/video corpus. Finally we need to integrate key constraints (e.g. *"every video is taken in some location"*, *"no two distinct videos are stored in the same file"*) or knowledge into the containment determinations (e.g. *"Manhattan is in New York"*).

As we extend FSA, it may yield insight into these problems as well as performance advantages. For example, sub-goal negation, in general, requires the canonical database approach to consider a combinatorial number of databases. Our approach might only require special non-spoiler gobblers linked to spoiler gobblers linked to a dead-end states. Also we suspect that encoding arithmetic constraints can be managed via branching over alternative variable orderings in our recursive automaton construction method. Finally, we speculate that our approach might be brought to more powerful automata to capture containment over ever more expressive query classes. It will be interesting to see how far we can get.

6   Conclusions

This paper evaluated a finite state automata approach to determining relational query containment. For conjunctive queries with limited set conditions the approach showed itself to be competitive with canonical database and theorem proving approaches. The approach still needs to be formally proven correct, and, if there are counterexamples, we must either extend the approach or develop natural assumptions to limit it to correct cases. Either way, the approach has been empirically validated under a fairly realistic corpus as well as for several special scalability tests. Future work will focus on extending the approach to cover more and more of the examples in our photo/video corpus (available at `sites.google.com/view/nli-corpora/`).

Acknowledgments

Umeå University masters student David Hansson built the initial CDB and TP implementations.

References

Foto Afrati, Matthew Damigos, and Manolis Gergatsoulis. 2010. Query containment under bag and bag-set semantics. *Inf. Process. Lett.*, 110(10):360–369.

Franz Baader, Ian Horrocks, and Ulrike Sattler. 2009. Description logics. In *Handbook on Ontologies*, pages 21–43.

Robert Baumgartner, Oliver Frölich, Georg Gottlob, Marcus Herzog, and Peter Lehmann. 2005. Integrating semi-structured data into business applications. In *Professional Knowledge Management, WM Kaiserslautern, Germany*, pages 469–482.

Henrik Björklund, Wim Martens, and Thomas Schwentick. 2011. Conjunctive query containment over trees. *J. Comput. Syst. Sci.*, 77(3):450–472.

Johan Bos and Tetsushi Oka. 2002. An inference-based approach to dialogue system design. In *COLING Taipei, Taiwan, August 24 - September 1, 2002*.

Ashok Chandra and Philip Merlin. 1977. Optimal implementation of conjunctive queries in relational databases. In *Proc. of STOC*, pages 77–90.

Sara Cohen. 2005. Containment of aggregate queries. *SIGMOD Record*, 34(1):77–85.

Ann Copestake and Karen Sparck Jones. 1990. Natural language interfaces to databases. *Knowledge Eng. Review*, 5(4):225–249.

Anthony Klug. 1988. On conjunctive queries containing inequalities. *J. ACM*, 35(1):146–160.

Alon Levy. 1999. Review - complexity of answering queries using materialized views. *ACM SIGMOD Digital Review*, 1.

Michael Minock. 2017. Cover: Covering the semantically tractable question. In *proceedings of EACL (Software Demonstrations)*, Valencia, April.

Stuart Shieber. 1993. The problem of logical-form equivalence. *Computational Linguistics*, 19(1):179–190.

Jeffrey Ullman. 1988. *Principles of Database and Knowledge-Base Systems*. Computer Science Press.

Jeffrey Ullman. 2000. Information integration using logical views. *Theor. Comput. Sci.*, 239(2):189–210.